Doing it Write

Writers' Library, Volume 2

C. Dennis Moore

Published by Shrine Keepers Publishing, 2018.

While every precaution has been taken in the preparation of this book, the publisher assumes no responsibility for errors or omissions, or for damages resulting from the use of the information contained herein.

DOING IT WRITE

First edition. January 29, 2018.

ISBN: 979-8231626007

Written by C. Dennis Moore.

Also by C. Dennis Moore

an Angel Hill short
Carlotta Valdez
Flagpole Sitta
Woolly Muffler
Private Helicopter
Problems and Bigger Ones
Jack the Lion
Old Hat
Terminal Annex
Wrecking Ball

Holiday Horrors
New Year's Day
Martin Luther King, Jr. Day
Groundhog Day
Ash Wednesday
Valentine's Day
Presidents' Day
Saint Patrick's Day

LATE-NIGHT DOUBLE FEATURES
Playground of the Gods
House of Limbs
Coming Down the Mountain
Revenge of the Roach King
Maggie Andrews Gets the Facts
Son of Man
The Legend of Mr. Cairo
Plaything
Illusion is a Synonym for Dream

Mini Collections
Five Fates
Five Fantasies
Five Furies

standalone shorts
Blood Bitch
Raw Materials
The Caterpillar
In the Town of Broken Dreams
Working for the Fat Man
The League of Liars
Biscuithead
The Fish in the Fields
The Envy of Falling Leaves
Road to Nowhere
The Timesmiths

The Angel Hill novels
The Man in the Window
The Ghosts of Mertland
The Flip
Housequake
The Third Floor 2: Suicide House
The Third Floor

The Monsters of Green Lake
The Werewolves of Green Lake
The Vampires of Green Lake
The Witches of Green Lake
The Demons of Green Lake

Writers' Library
10 Writing Prompts That Work (and the stories to prove it)
Doing it Write
Writing Rules
Shut Up and Write

Standalone
Aftermath
Terrible Thrills
Bloodletting
Dancing on a Razorblade
The Dichotomy of Monsters

Love Jones
What the Blind Man Saw
Camdigan
Kung Fu Sasquatch
Science Fiction Double Feature (Foodies of Mars variant)
Science Fiction Double Feature (Purple Haze variant)
So Quake With Fear, You Tiny Fools!
The Nightmare Corridor
Inside
The Only Way Out is Through
The Organ Grinder
Revelations
Alter
The Lonely Man: Road to The Third Floor 2
Red House
Fluke
The American Way Vs. Dr. Brain
Welcome to the Trust

DEDICATION

For David Bain.

INTRODUCTION

• • • •

I'VE BEEN WRITING SINCE 1991, and, barring a few periods here and there where life got in the way, I've written pretty much every day. I'm no expert. I don't think any writer with a sense of reality would ever consider themselves an expert. But we do gain knowledge and experience over time, if we're paying attention. And that knowledge and experience can always be used to help others who are going through the things we've already gone through.

So I wrote this book for them. For the new writers who hope to avoid the pitfalls and mistakes us long-timers made along the way, and for veteran writers who've forgotten why they fell in love with writing in the first place. It happens.

But like I said, I'm no expert. While the sentiments and ideas in this book are mine, the structure is not.

I had gotten to a point in my life and my writing career where I felt I needed some direction. I was writing, but not really loving the process as much as I used to. My day job was wearing me out, and it seemed no matter how much time and effort I put into writing, it just wasn't paying off like it used to. I had gone from making my mortgage payment for well over a year on my book sales to ... well, being glad I still had a day job, and I was getting pretty disillusioned with the whole thing. So I turned to other, smarter and more successful people than me. I found this list of twenty-five books to read to help you achieve success in life and business. At the top of that list was AWAKEN THE GIANT WITHIN by Tony Robbins. I'd been seeing his ads on TV since I was 18 or 19, but had never read any of his books. I'd heard a few interviews with him and he'd always seemed so confident in his approach. I checked online and saw I could get a hardcover copy of his book for a few bucks. I ordered it, got it, and started reading it immediately.

And then, in the middle of the first chapter, a strange thing happened. I was inspired. Not by what he was saying, but by how easily I found I was able to take that information and adapt it to writers and writing. After finishing that first chapter I immediately went to my computer and wrote a blog post called DECIDE TO CHANGE THE COURSE OF YOUR LIFE.

I did this for one reason. I have a close friend, another writer, who is ten times the writer I am, but hadn't published anything in over a year at that time. So I thought maybe if I take the message Robbins was laying down in that first chapter and show my friend how that information can be adapted to writers and inspire them to make the changes they needed to make in order to be the writer they wanted to be … maybe it would be just the thing he needed to get back to work.

And then it happened again the next day when I read chapter two. And it kept happening. Every day as I read through this book, I kept finding ways to adapt his message to writers, and writing blogs about it. I found I was addicted to the process and, instead of reading the book for my OWN benefit, I was reading to see how I could use that information to help other writers.

Soon it was almost all I was thinking about. I was excited every morning to get to that day's chapter so I could see how else I could use my new knowledge to help my colleagues.

And that, eventually, led to this book. I had no intention at first of ever publishing those posts in a book. After all, who the hell am I that I should deign to say I know any better than anyone else. Well, I don't. And any writer who tells you he does, run away, because he's 1) full of shit, or 2) an idiot. Most likely he's an idiot who is full of shit.

Every writer's path is different, but the tips and suggestions laid out in this book are here to help guide you in the most common ways writers can use to find their voice and/or their drive.

Each chapter is adapted from the original blog post with updates and revisions for the purposes of this book, and they're designed to be taken one day at a time. Because change is never immediate, it's something we have to work toward one step at a time. Otherwise, we'll change for a few days, but then slip right back into our old habits. So don't feel you have to read this book all at once. You could, it's only about 31,000 words, but I think you'll get more benefit from it reading one chapter a day and adapting what you find there to your own life and your own craft. And it's not just for writers, this information is good for ANY creative person, whether artist, musician, filmmaker, or whatever. I talk most about writing because I'm a writer.

Before we get into the meat of the book, though, there are a few chapters up front about setting up your writing space and getting organized and ready to write. These are tips picked up from over 25 years of writing, concerning office space, desk set-up, and time management, none of which can be ignored if you want to be successful. Do not underestimate the importance of workspace and time management, please.

So we'll get through those first and, once your workspace is set up and you've got your writing schedule all lined up, then we'll dive into the motivation portion of the book.

Without further ado, let's start with where you choose to do your work.

WRITING IN YOUR OWN SPACE

. . . .

"A WOMAN MUST HAVE MONEY and a room of her own if she is to write fiction."—Virginia Woolf

This is 100% accurate. You have to do it. And I get that not everyone has a separate room in their house where they can go and close the door and work in solitude, but if you want to do this job and do it seriously, you HAVE to set up a space that is just yours, and when you're in that space, no one is allowed to intrude. It can be a corner of the bedroom, or the dining room table during certain hours of the day. Honestly, though, you'd be better off in a closet. A closed door does wonders for the creative mind. I write at home alone for most of the day, but even when I'm the only one in the house, I close my office door. It's a mental trick to shut out the world and really focus. I've never understood how people are able to take their laptop to a coffee shop and create anything of value surrounded by other people. That's not to say it's wrong, or they can't do it, I just don't get it. A writer—or musician or painter, whatever your creative outlet of choice—needs to have a space dedicated to that thing. It's the first step in taking it seriously as opposed to seeing it as simply a hobby.

And then, once you've cordoned off your area for WORK, personalize it. Put up a picture, place an action figure next to your computer, or buy a chair that is just for writing. Whatever you do, personalize that space so everyone else in the house knows this is MY spot where I work.

If you're still trying to create at the kitchen table while the family is in the living room watching television all night, or worse, you're huddled one on end of the couch with your laptop while they're playing videogames two feet from you, take this one important step and get the hell out. Find a room, ANY room, with a door, even the aforementioned closet. Tape a sign to the outside of that door that reads "Unless it's bleeding, it can wait!", and then close that door and don't open it again until you're done for the day. You have to do it. You'll thank me later.

FIX YO LIFE UP, A DISCUSSION ABOUT ORGANIZATION FOR WRITERS

• • • •

LET'S TALK ABOUT ORGANIZATION. I'm a huge list maker. I love lists and systems. I make lists for everything. Right now I have four lists taped to the side of my desk. One is a blog schedule, so when I actually have time to blog on a regular basis, but have no idea what to blog about, this list gives me a guideline to follow (don't bother checking previous entries; I did specify "when I have time" and most nights I pack corn dogs for 10 hours). Another list is the Superhero TV shows I want to watch, because there are so many I have to write them down so I don't forget about any of them. I try to watch one every afternoon while I eat before I go to work. At first, I was binge-watching, but then realized I'm so far behind on some of them, why not just watch one episode every week. That's what I have to do with the ones I watch live, and that's what I'd be doing if these weren't on Netflix. So right now, that list is "Arrow" (finished season 2), "Daredevil" (all caught up). "Agents of SHIELD" (finished season 2), "Flash" (current, watch live), "Gotham" (finished season 2), "Supergirl" (current, watch live), "Legends of Tomorrow" (current, watch live). As shows rotate in and out of season on Netflix, this list has become a bit outdated, but as I worked through it, I found I needed it less and less and was watching particular shows on particular days.

Another list reads only "Netflix, DVD, King". This was my movie review list. I made this list a few years ago when I working noon to 8 and could get up at 4:00 and do some writing. This gave me time to write AND do movie reviews, which I've always loved doing. But there were so many options. I have collected hundreds of horror movies on

DVD, but there's also Netflix, and I'm also trying to work through the Stephen King movie library. So I made a list and rotated through it. Simple.

The last list is the longest. It's the list of upcoming stories I'm going to write. It's 15 titles long and the first two are crossed out. Again, it comes down to having so many to do and needing a way to sort them out.

I've just spent more of the last two mornings than I care to admit watching organizational skills for writers videos on YouTube, and holy crap! I don't know how some people get anything done. They're either too laser focused, to the point they're obviously making their system more complicated than necessary as a means of wasting time so they can avoid actually WRITING, or they're so disorganized and scatter-brained as they're filming that there's no way in hell I'd ever take their advice.

This is all a very long-winded way of saying that, personally, I think, as a writer, there are only two organizational tools you need: a piece of paper and a pen. If you can't get your shit together using these two items, then you've got bigger problems. Some writers I know use apps to organize their lives, but, again, this is just making a bigger deal out of something than it needs to be. If you want to make a note about something, make a note. Simple. If you want to track sales, track sales. If you want to create a character, create a character. There is literally not one part of planning and organization a writer is going to have to do that can't be done with pen and paper.

Some writers use notebooks, some are more haphazard and use whatever random scrap of paper they can find. I've been both of these people in my 26 years as a writer. I find notebooks are definitely the way to go. And, no, you don't have to buy a fancy leather-bound one with gold leaf pages and a silk bookmark stitched in. Not saying you can't, but you'll take the exact same notes in a $1 spiral from the Dollar Store.

Lists and systems have helped more over the years than I think anything or anyone else has. And that's no offense to the friends and mentors I've had over the years, their help is also very much appreciated. But the lists and systems keep it all straight.

As a beginning writer, I found, as I think most writers do, that I had more ideas than I had time to write them all. So what does a person do when they're already in the middle of something but don't want to lose this other idea?

I wrote it down. Usually the title, if there was one, but sometimes just a few words to give the general idea of the story. For example, my short story, "The Foodies of Mars" was nothing more than a note which read "DNA gene therapy". For "The Envy of Falling Leaves", it was "aging immortal". I made a list I titled LIST in my word processor and eventually had pages and pages of story titles and ideas. That's all well and good, but how do you know which one to work on next? I could always take the simple route and just work my way down the list. But that's not what I did.

Instead I printed the list and cut up all the titles, so each idea was on a separate slip of paper. I put these into a small box and when it was time to write a new story, I'd give the box a shake and blindly draw the next title. That was the story I wrote next. I've always believed in chance being a big factor for me. Or rather faith. I had faith that, whatever story I was writing next was the story I was supposed to write next. And it always worked out.

Years later, as I collected a rather large pile of stories, finished and not finished, I had to develop another system to work through them. Enter the file holder and the rotation. I had one of these and used it to hold the files I kept my physical copies in. ALWAYS keep physical copies. What are you insane, relying on computers and electronics? Don't you know those things die all the time? With my old word processor I once lost nearly 70 pages when my foot hit the cord and knocked it out of the wall one night. Always keep physical copies!

Anyway, I used this to hold my files. I'd write a first draft and into the organizer it went. Then I'd pull another random title from another small box labeled "revisions". I'd revise and edit that story, and into the organizer it would go. I'd do a new first draft and into the organizer. Then a revision. Then a first draft. Once it was full, I'd start at the front and work through them again. The first drafts would become revisions and move to the back of the organizer. The revisions would, hopefully, get to a point I thought they were publishable, and I'd submit them. This system worked for me for years. Eventually I dropped it, but not because it stopped working, I just stopped using it. But it worked so well because it forced me to give those brilliant first drafts that I thought were amazing when I finished them a chance to rest. And it made sure I didn't leave those stories that were less than they could be in a file gathering dust somewhere. I know my penchant for moving on and leaving the old stories behind me and I had to find a way to overcome that. This system worked perfectly for that.

There are others. Christ, I've come up with systems for just about anything you can imagine. My entire day is scheduled to the hour (this is one of the many many many reasons I loathe my day job so much; we go in at the same time but we leave when we're done. That's either too much unscheduled time or too little and my brain doesn't like that). I've got systems for what books I read next. Sometimes, if I'm feeling like I need some music, I've got systems for that. My daughter and I both have a system—we adopted the same exact system independently of each other—for what to wear the next day.

And in all that time, I've never needed anything more high-tech than a pen and a piece of paper.

If any writer tells you that you need this app or that app or this device or that gadget to organize your writing or your day, they're an idiot, and you can tell them I said so.

TAKING TIME TO MAKE TIME, SCHEDULING YOUR YEAR IN REVERSE.

. . . .

I WANT TO TALK ABOUT scheduling. Why it's important, and how to do it right.

First, why it's important. Because we're all busy people with full lives, things to do, and people who will try to distract you and knock you off your game. Even if they don't mean to, they will. Things come up, family obligations or you lose an entire day of writing because you have a flat tire and have to get it replaced so you can make it to work that night. Stuff happens, and when it does it can be hard getting back into the groove and the routine once that routine is broken. And I'm a person who thrives on routine. I have little enough time in the day, what with spending 9-10 of those hours packing hot dogs 6 days a week, to waste it on NOT doing the things I want to do. And my first year at this job, I spent so much time trying to acclimate myself to the new schedule—I hadn't worked a night job in 15 years—that I didn't finish anything in the first 6 or 7 months I worked there. I wrote stuff, I just never finished it. I'd get the first draft out and then move on and never come back to it.

So I made a decision at the end of 2014. In 2015, I was going to publish one title a month all year. I knew that making this plan—and stating it publicly so I had accountability—would get me off my ass and WRITING. But first I had to have a plan, and schedule the titles so I knew when I was writing what and allowed myself enough time to finish them.

When you make a plan this big, that covers an entire year, you have to start BIG and work your way backward. So I started with 2015. Okay, one year, 12 months, 12 titles to publish.

That means I publish one new title every month. So that gives me 4 weeks every month to get the next title ready to go.

I looked back at the projects I had started and not finished in 2014 and saw I had a good 6 of them. So that's half the year taken care of. But I didn't want to publish all of them upfront and leave the latter half of the year blank. What if something came up? Something big. And anyway, how sure was I that I could write 6 new titles in 6 months, one after another? Not very.

So instead, I spread those 6 almost-ready titles throughout the year, with an empty month in between them. So, yeah, I still had to write 6 new titles that year, but instead of having only a month to do it, I actually had 7 weeks. Because these 6 almost-ready titles, the hard part was done. All I had to do was edit and polish, and they were ready to go. I could do that in a week. So that left the 3 weeks of that month, and 4 weeks of the next month, to write my next title. Plenty of time.

This is how I got through 2015. I'd spend a week revising and polishing a first draft, and at the end of that week, publish it. Then I had 7 weeks to write, revise, polish, and publish something new. Then I spent a week revising and polishing a first draft. I alternated back and forth and, at the end of 2015, I had 12 new titles online. I could never have done that without planning and scheduling.

I started big, 2015. Then worked my way back and scheduled January, then February, then March, and on and on to December.

From there, I scheduled the weeks. The first week of January, I revised and polished. Then the rest of January and all of February, I wrote something new, polished it, published it. Then the first week of March ... you get the idea.

But from there I had to schedule even further, and even smaller. The days.

Sure, I had all week to revise and polish, but the formatting and publishing can take a while, so really I only had 4 days to do that, and the formatting and publishing—both ebook and print formats—would take up all of Friday. I wasn't spending a lot of time in my office on the weekends; it was the only time I was home and I used it to catch up on all the things I didn't get done throughout the week. And, again, if I hadn't scheduled these things, if I'd just left the entire year up to chance with the only plan being publish a new title every month, there would have been chaos. I wouldn't have finished 12 new titles, I would have done the 6 I had in first draft already—MAYBE—and possibly another 1 or 2 new ones throughout the year.

And this is why scheduling and planning is so important if you want to turn this writing thing you do in your off time into a career. You can't go at it randomly. It's a business. More than that, it's a JOB. Your friends and family may not see it that way, but you HAVE TO. And you have to approach it like one. Your boss at your day job doesn't let you just come in whenever you have time, get done whatever small amount you can accomplish in a couple hours, and then leave because something came up. God I wish mine did, though. That would be pretty sweet.

And if your boss won't let you do that at one job, why should the boss—you—at the other job? I'm not going to go into scheduling your day so you have time to write every day. Not in this post anyway. Maybe in a later one. But you know your day, you know where you do and don't have time. Writing is like anything else in life, if it's important enough to you, you'll find the time to do it. Hopefully this helped anyone out there struggling with time constraints and lack of motivation.

ATTACK OF THE BAGUA!!!

• • • •

LET'S GET ORGANIZED.

There's only one office tip I want to give out before we move to the desk, but it's an important tip and will help not only your productivity, but your mindset as well.

DO NOT set your desk so your back is to the door. This will make you feel like everything is happening "behind your back" and your work won't get your full concentration. You have to be able to see people coming into the office at you. If your space is just too small and you don't have a choice, put a mirror over the desk so you can see behind you.

Now on to the desk.

I spent a lot of years working in and around offices and I've seen a LOT of peoples' desks and how they personalize and organize them. I've also seen a lot of writers' desks and sometimes it's a wonder they get anything done. Although, to be fair, I've also heard it said several times that a messy desk can be more creative. So there's that.

But if you have a hard time working through the clutter, here are a few tips that can help you set up your desk for maximum productivity.

One: Sit in the command position. This goes back to desk placement. You don't have to face the door directly—in fact, it's a good idea if you don't. If you want to follow feng shui guidelines, "you will receive the full force of energy coming into the room and you may feel confused or agitated." From my experience, it's just as much a distraction as having the door at your back. Every little creak or cough, you're going to be looking up to make sure nothing is coming at you. You want to sit where you have command of the room. So sit either facing the room, but with the door not directly in front of you, or sit facing the wall with the door off to the side—again, not facing you. You don't want that energy coming directly at you.

Second: Get a solid desk. No glass tops. Again, if you want the feng shui principle, a glass top allows the creative energy to flow down and disappear. From a realistic standpoint, they're just fragile. They require too much cleaning, they scratch too easily, and they break a lot easier than a solid wood-top desk. So stop thinking you're fancy with your all metal and glass desk, and get a grown-up's desk.

Third: Get a supportive chair. If you're going to make a living sitting down all day, you have to be comfortable doing it. And if you're like me and you work a lot of late nights and you're going to occasionally doze off at your desk, you might as well be comfortable doing it.

Fourth: Remember the 50-/50 rule. Your desktop should be made up for 50% work and personal materials (computer, papers, files, family pictures, personal knick knacks, etc), and 50% clean desk top. Obviously, when you're in the middle of a project, your desk is going to get messy. Especially if you have one of those comfortable chairs. God, it's SO MUCH EASIER to just set things aside and let them pile up. There's nothing wrong with this at all. Goes back to a messy desk being more creative. But at the very least, clean your desk off before you start a new project. What I've been doing, since things tend to pile up on my desk every day or two, BEFORE I EVEN SIT DOWN FOR THE DAY, I clean it off, put away the papers or books or Cds that have begun to pile up. I clean it off before I've even gotten comfortable, otherwise it's just not going to happen that day.

Fifth, and this is the most interesting part, I think: when setting up your desk, use the key areas of the bagua. What the WHAT, you're saying!

A bagua is "one of the main tools used in feng shui to analyze the energy of any given space, be it home, office or garden. Basically, bagua is the feng shui energy map of your space that shows you which areas of your home or office are connected to specific areas of your life."

The bagua is laid out generally in a grid much like the Brady Bunch opening with these key areas:

Wealth Fame Love

Family Children

Knowledge Career Helpful People

The center of the desk closest to your chair is the career spot. This is, generally, where you put your computer to do your work. You'll fill the other areas of the bagua with things that bring that specific area to mind. For example the Love and Children area of my desk holds pictures of my kids. Unfortunately, my desk is offset, so the open area where I sit is to the left, in the knowledge area, while the right side of the desk is drawers. So while I can't use the bagua the way it's laid out to set up my own desk, I can adapt the parts of it that I CAN reach. The knowledge area is also where my phone goes when I'm writing. The Fame area is where I keep a few important books: The Seven Habits of Highly Effective People (which I WILL get around to reading one day, I swear), "642 Things to Write About", the Writer's Workbook I published last year, and "Good Advice on Writing". My desk faces a wall—with the door to my office to my right, on the same wall—so the wall in front of me, the family and wealth area, is plastered with more pictures of my kids, as well as my lists for what projects are coming up, and a "heart, horror, spectacle" reminder taped to the top. If and when I ever get a new desk, I'll be looking for one with the career area in the middle, but for now, I spent so much money on this desk and I've only had it three years, I can't justify getting rid of it just now. Plus, I love this desk. It's got a ton of storage and allows me to decorate it with things that are personal to me, like my Carrie White and Regan McNeil figures, my Hellboy piggy bank, my plush Leatherface, my Garden Rain candle, and the Bane figure my son got me years ago. It actually used to be a lot more cluttered, but I've pared down greatly and now only keep things on my desk that inspire me.

There's a ton more information out there for proper feng shui desk set up. If you want more help in this area, contact me and I'll be happy to help.

• • • •

THIS IS WHERE WE GET to the heart of the book. These next twenty-five chapters are going to get you organized, motivated, fired up and in the state of mind to write yourself to the life you've always wanted. And while I make NO promises about SELLING that work once it's published, this book will definitely help you be more productive and sure of yourself as a writer.

Whatever problems your facing when it comes to finding time or faith in yourself to sit down and do the work, this book will help you with that.

This book isn't meant strictly for beginners. Any writer who's been writing for any length of time can use the tips in here to help recharge their batteries, find their center, and remember why it is they wanted to do this.

Let's get started with something simple. Just make a choice.

1. DECIDE TO CHANGE THE COURSE OF YOUR LIFE.

. . . .

TODAY I GOT UP AND decided to brush my teeth. Then I decided to wash my work clothes—my PJ pants, my sweater and my hoodie. Then I decided to do a little reading before getting my day officially started. I decided to make coffee instead of drinking water. I decided to have a cookie. I decided to let the dog out now instead of waiting until later. Then I decided to sit down at my computer and get started. I looked at what I wrote yesterday and decided, those 1000 words I wanted to write today? Yeah, I was gonna make that happen.

Every decision you make has consequences, good or bad. I can accept gum disease or I can fight it. I can feel good in my fresh, clean work clothes, or I can feel like crap in the hoodie I wore last night and the night before (I work in 30 degree coolers every night). I could do something other than write those 1000 words and NOT make any progress on this current story or I can sit down, focus, and DO THE WORK. Either way, it was my decision.

Writing is seldom easy. It takes time, it takes focus, and sometimes there are just so many other things we'd RATHER be doing. Sometimes there are things we're supposed to be doing. I should really be getting my daughter to come down and cut my hair for me, but I'm deciding to do this first.

I will assume most of the people reading this are grown adults and that means there's no one MAKING you do anything during the course of your day. Nothing you don't LET them make you do, that is. At the end of the day, though, each decision you make is yours and yours alone. So YOU decide if you get those words written. YOU decide if you finish that story on time. YOU decide if you write anything at all from one day to the next. Just you.

Now, these decisions may piss some people off when they don't fall in line with what THEY want to happen, but that's a decision, too. YOUR decision to follow your course, THEIR decision to let it piss them off. And those decisions have consequences, as well.

In early 1991, I DECIDED to start writing that story that had been plaguing me every night for weeks when I closed to my eyes to go to sleep. I could have decided not to write that story. It might have gone away, eventually, and my life might have followed a different course. A better course? Who can say? But I did decide to start writing that story. I could have decided writing it was enough and never shown it to anyone. Instead I decided to show my high school composition teacher and she encouraged me to keep going. I could have decided to ignore her and give up. Instead I decided I wanted to finish that story—which eventually turned into my novel THE MAN IN THE WINDOW (which you can get free at https://www.instafreebie.com/free/MLCIv).

Decide where you want your life to go, and then decide what's the best path to get there. It might not be the popular path, but only you can decide if it's worth taking to get where you want to go. Decisions have consequences, but doing nothing, deciding NOT to decide has consequences of its own.

I would LOVE to get another hour or two of sleep before work today. I'm deciding to be productive and get things done instead.

2. FINDING PLEASURE THROUGH PAIN

. . . .

SEVERAL YEARS AGO, we remodeled our kitchen. And by remodeled I mean we gutted it. The only thing in there from the original kitchen is the floor and the light fixture. Everything else went. And holy God it sucked. I don't ever want to hang another cabinet in my life. But, MAN, the result was so much better than what was there before. It was hard, it was exhausting, and I was so sore from it. But it was totally worth it to walk into that kitchen at the end and see the result of that hard work.

I've been saying it for years: writing is hard. You're a few thousand words into your latest story and it's time to sit down and do the words for the day, but something inside says that's gonna be hard today. The next scene isn't crystallized in your head and the words are gonna come slow. Why not do something else? Something fun. Let's watch some YouTube videos. Or let's take a little nap instead. You can write it tomorrow. In fact, that extra day will give your head time to catch up so when you DO sit down to write, you'll be fired up and ready to go.

That's your brain trying to trick you into opting for pleasure over pain. The pleasure, albeit short lived, of a quick YouTube marathon or a peek at Twitter over the temporary pain of trying to get these words out when you know damn well the pleasure at the end of that, another 1000, another 2000 words, is going to get you that much closer to finishing that first draft.

People so often take the immediate pleasure route instead of facing that temporary pain when the pleasure at the end of it is going to be so much bigger than that immediate one. What does a few YouTube videos do to further your writing career? How is a glance at your

Twitter feed going to make you any money selling more books? Especially if we do those things at the expense of actual writing?

Nothing worth having was ever GIVEN, it was EARNED through struggle and hardship. You don't lose a few pounds by sitting around eating cake. God, what a world that would be, though. Instead you have to eat the right foods and get off your dead ass. Yeah, it sucks, but at the end, when your body is in the shape you want it to be, the shape that says you need to show this off to people, the loss of a few Twinkies, the time spent on the treadmill or with the weights is totally worth it.

Every short story I've ever written, every novel, over 26 years, I had to sit down and DO it. So many times I'd have rather been reading or napping or at the movies with my family. ANYTHING else. But I sacrificed a little immediate pain and eventually, especially when THE THIRD FLOOR took off like it did, that little bit of immediate pain turned into days of pleasure when I was able to take my family on a mini vacation and, later, spend two days at an amusement park and, again later, get everyone tickets to see our favorite comedians when their tour came through town. The struggles to get those words down paid off.

There were times in the early days when my son was only two or three and I'd come home from work and head immediately upstairs to my office to write for two hours. He'd run after me and want to come with and I had to stop him and tell him he couldn't come. It killed me, but it had to be done because I wanted a career as a writer, hopefully one that would give me even MORE time with him. It hurt like hell to do that to the kid, but it was for a bigger reward later. And considering what writing has afforded me with my kids since then, I'd do it again.

Your body and mind are naturally going to lean toward the path of least resistance and there's nothing less resistant than NOT doing something, so of course that route always looks better. But you have to ask yourself what's more important to my personal growth, a little pleasure now through an absence of pain, or a lot of pleasure later by going through a small fire right now?

Sit down, write the book, get the words down. There are going to be days they fight back, but through practice we gain experience and experience ALWAYS makes things easier.

The real question is, what's more important to YOU?

3. I WANT TO BELIEVE!

• • • •

WHAT DO YOU BELIEVE?

I believe I can write a short story in a week. I believe I can average 1000 words an hour, and I believe that, when I'm REALLY into it, I can do it in half that time. I believe these things because I've done them.

There was a time I believed I would never write fiction. I had tried several times in my younger days and could never get past the first page. There was a time I believed I could never be a voracious reader because in grade school I was always the last to finish in Reading class when we had to read the story to ourselves. Now I have a library in my house with 11 bookshelves stuffed full of books and I'm almost never seen outside my house without something to read at hand. How did I change that belief that I'd never be a voracious reader? I read.

Beliefs are precarious things, subject to change on a dime. Surely you've heard the story of Roger Bannister and the four-minute mile? If not, in summary: For years, it was a commonly held belief that running a mile in four minutes was simply impossible. And then Roger Bannister applied himself and did the impossible. Once that barrier had been broken, it began to happen more and more frequently and within a few years of Bannister having changed the commonly held belief, hundreds of people had run a mile in four minutes.

Whatever you believe today, you might just believe the exact opposite tomorrow.

But what about those beliefs that are based on nothing more than fear or self-doubt?

There's the writer who says I don't have time to write. They spend all day at work, slaving away and then, by the time the end of the day rolls around, they were so busy keeping up with their hectic lives, they simply didn't have time to sit for thirty minutes and WRITE. But I bet you they had time to Tweet. And I bet you their Facebook status is updated. They don't have time to write because they BELIEVE they don't have time. They take a look around at their lives and see the kids who need a ride, the spouse who needs this or that, the dog who needs to be walked, and they just don't have time for anything else.

But I also bet if you look into this writer's list of credits, you'll see PLENTY of finished stories and novels. They HAVE written. Obviously they had time. So what's changed?

A schedule change, a job change, a shift change, a change in the family dynamic, these things have a tendency to throw one off-balance and some people have a hard time finding that rhythm again. Ergo: they just don't have time. That's their belief, anyway.

But remember, beliefs are precarious things. I started a new first draft this morning and at one time that would have scared the hell out of me. But since I've tackled so many first drafts over 26 years of writing, I BELIEVE I can tackle, and finish, another one. The next time I sit down to start a new novel, I'll be intimidated by the length. But a look at my shelves and all the other novels I've finished will reinforce my belief that I can do it. I won't go so far as to say you can do ANYTHING you believe you can—we'd all be flying and shooting beams from our eyes—but I will say that if you believe you CAN'T do something, then you absolutely cannot do it.

So how do you change your beliefs?

1) Get your brain to associate pain with the current belief. "I don't have time to write, so I won't write" turns into "I'm stuck in this dead-end job I hate with no way out" turns into, "Okay, so maybe I can carve out a LITTLE time to write. I can get up a little earlier, stay up a little later, dictate on the drive to work, write on my lunch break."

2) Then you have to associate pleasure to the idea of the new belief. Look to all the self publishing authors out there who had that one hit and were able to quit their day jobs and write full time. You know you want that life. Imagine it. Put yourself in their place.

3) Next, create doubt. Take a serious look at your daily routine. How much time are you wasting on YouTube? A lot, I'd bet. How much time are you spending watching television? I dig a good Seinfeld rerun as much as the next guy, but you've seen that episode and that's 30 minutes you could be writing. I could do 1000 words in 30 minutes. Not every time, but I can definitely do 500 in that time. Are you SURE you don't have ANY time to write? You have to question those beliefs because doing that enough times, sooner or later, you'll begin to doubt, and doubt, as Megan Phelps-Roper can tell you, is how we get our brains to start adopting some NEW beliefs.

We'll never change our behavior and our patterns as long as we hold to the old beliefs. And if you're constantly telling yourself I don't have time for this, or I'll never be able to finish something like that, you're on the wrong end of it. Save the cheerleader, save the world. Change your beliefs, change your life. The process might not always be simple, there might be people standing in your way, trying to hinder your personal growth, but if you don't start with YOURSELF, there'll never be any personal growth in the first place. Believe that, and it's true.

4. CAN YOU SPARE SOME CHANGE?

• • • •

FROM JAN 2000 TO JAN 2003 I worked in the electronics warehouse at Altec, maker of aerial and derrick trucks the world over. I was good at that job. I took what had been believed to be a two-man job and, within 6 months, proved one person could do it alone, so they moved my boss out to the production floor, hired me full time, and I ran the hell out of that warehouse until the company hit a rough patch and, on the third round of layoffs, I got caught in the net. It sucked. It was one of the lowest points in my life. But one thing I learned there, a lesson I've taken with me ever since, was something Altec did as a company, something they'd learned from the Japanese, called kaizen, which translates to "continuous improvement."

Altec didn't make company-wide changes overnight, they implemented small changes here and there, improving things as they went. I've said writing is hard? CHANGE is hard. When you're set in your ways, when you have a routine, man it's hard to get out of that mindset. And if you try to do it all at once, it's damn near impossible.

This is where the kaizen philosophy comes into play. By making small changes day to day, we can slowly, gradually, make the improvements we need to make.

I like this process because it's also exactly how writing works. No story is finished the moment you start it, no matter how clear it is in your head. We chip away at it every day, adding a little here and there. I started a new first draft yesterday and when I sat down at my computer and opened a new document, I had no words.

I started the story and one word at a time turned into one sentence at a time turned into one paragraph at a time until around half an hour later, I had 1049 words. That's not going to finish the story, not by a long shot. All I'd done was write the opening scene.

But I could pick it up again today and do a little more. And do a little more tomorrow. And a little more the next day. I hope to get the first draft finished by Friday and I'm feeling pretty confident that, one word at a time, I can make that happen. Today I did over 1600 words. Tomorrow I may only get 1000 again, but that's cool because every little bit helps in changing this blank page to a finished short story.

I've been a devotee of kaizen for almost 17 years now and still use it in almost every facet of my life. From what route to work is the best to making sure I have time for writing AND time to spend with my daughter every day before work, I'm constantly working on things, making small adjustments where I see them in order to make things flow as smoothly as possible.

One HUGE help in this regard is my calendar. For the longest time I knew I only had so many hours in the day to get things done so I just tried to cram as much in as I could and hope for the best. But it never failed that, every night at work I would remember something I had wanted to do that day but forgot. And I ALWAYS ran out of time and didn't get as much with my daughter as I'd wanted.

I started off texting reminders to myself but of course sometimes forgot to check those. I moved to jotting down reminders when I got home from work at night, but sometimes things fall off your desk and you forget or just neglect to pick them up, so I started writing them in a notebook. But I'm left-handed and spirals dig into my wrist when I write in them, so I wasn't doing that quite as regularly as I should have. And then I remembered I had a calendar shoved into my desk drawer. The spaces aren't that big and I'm a sloppy writer, so I can't fit too many things into each space, but that works out perfectly because it keeps me from overextending myself every day. Instead, every day when I get done working and am about to sit down to lunch and Mystery Science Theatre with my daughter, I take a minute to write down the next 5-6 things I want to get done the next day. I do it early, while they're still on my mind, so I don't forget until I get to work anymore.

And now, through making those small changes here and there as I progressed, I've got a nearly ironclad system for scheduling my day and maximizing what time I have before it's off to work again.

And the beauty of kaizen is it applies to every aspect of life. From relationships, to education, to finances, to health, to ... everything. Little changes, incremental changes, CONSTANT changes as you go will eventually result in a life well lived. What do you want to change? Start today with ONE change.

5. THE TRUTH ON A SHAMPOO BOTTLE: LATHER, RINSE, REPEAT. THEN CONDITION.

. . . .

WHEN YOU PUT A NEW set of strings on your guitar, you have to tune it up, then stretch the strings and tune it again. Then stretch the strings and tune it again. Why? You have to condition the strings to be at that tension level.

When it's time for the dog to go back into his kennel at night, I stand up from the couch, click my tongue, and he knows to go in. This simple, unspoken command wasn't bred into him, I conditioned him to know that means it's time to go in.

In the great war between inspiration and discipline, conditioning plays a huge role.

When I was younger and just starting out writing, I thought you had to be inspired to write. And when you felt that spark of inspiration, stop everything and run immediately to pen and paper! I'm inspired, dammit, you can't stifle my creativity! How very DARE you!

Well, that doesn't always work. Sometimes you're on the line packing hot dogs and you can't just stop, take off your gloves, pull pen and paper from your pocket and write something down. You're probably not even supposed to have pen and paper in the clean room. And then on the opposite end, sometimes the words just aren't coming and inspiration is nowhere to be found.

So we condition ourselves to write. For over a decade, my routine was to get up at 4:00 AM, write for two hours, go to work. Then I suddenly found myself without a job for several months and I had all day. But my mind was already conditioned and it wanted to be writing no later than 4:30, and if I hadn't got started by 5:00 at the latest, the entire day was shot.

It took a while, slowly starting later and later, writing for longer periods of time, later into the day until one day my mind was finally at a place where I could write AFTER the sun comes up, AFTER everyone else is awake and the world is in motion.

By repeating the same steps, sitting down and writing, my mind was conditioned. Trent Reznor said in a song, "I believe I can see the future cuz I repeat the same routine," but for me, routine is a way of life. If you're waiting to write that novel until you're INSPIRED, you'll die with an unwritten novel in you, I promise. Because inspiration is a fickle bitch. But discipline and conditioning get the job done every time.

So how do you condition yourself? By doing the work.

Remember Pavlov's dogs? He rang a bell every day at feeding time and soon the dogs began to salivate at the sound of the bell, whether food was coming or not. Their neural pathways had been altered.

Michael Merzenich did a study with monkeys in which he mapped a touch-activated area of one monkey's brain and then taught the monkey to use a particular finger in order to get food. When he later mapped that area again, he discovered the part of the monkey's brain associated with touch had grown by almost 600%. Through repetition and conditioning, the neural pathways of the monkey's brain grew stronger until it was ingrained in this monkey to use that finger in order to be fed. This is the same principle you'll use to condition your brain to know when it's time to write, it's time to write.

This works best, of course, if you're able to write at the same time every day. Even if it's only for a few minutes at a time. Find those times and condition your brain to know at these times you're going to be writing. So be prepared to make with the words.

Back before I had conditioned myself, I would find I had thirty minutes to kill and nothing to do, so let's try to write something.

Sometimes it worked but a lot of times it didn't. It was only when I picked a time of day to write, whether before or after work, and sat down at that same time every day, day after day, that I started having fewer and fewer days with no words written. It's the same as working out ANY muscle. You do it enough, stretch it, work it, use it consistently, that you start to see real physical progress.

Your mind is a muscle and like every other muscle it can be dormant and grow weak or you can exercise it to the point it's like a rock, a big hulking rock ready to smash anything in its path. When Merzenich's monkey was trained NOT to use that finger anymore, subsequent brain mappings showed those neural pathways had started to shrink. I've made a consistent effort to be at my desk at the same time every day for 25 years—that time changes depending on my job and what shift I'm working, but since I don't change jobs very often, I don't change writing schedules very often either—and I'd put my conditioning up against even the most dedicated writers out there.

If you're a struggling writer trying to fight through the haze of writer's block—another problem I very very rarely face; my brain knows that between these hours I've set aside, I'm writing—or lack of inspiration, know that there's hope. When you take writing seriously, treat it like a second—or third—job, and give it the respect and time you would to any other job, when you TAKE the time every day to shut out the world and the people in it and just WRITE, the words will come. I promise you they'll come.

And when you've got family or friends who give you a hard time about how come I can't get hold of you at this time every day, well they can be conditioned too. At the same time you're conditioning YOUR mind to be a working writer, you're conditioning THEIR minds to leave you the hell alone during that time you've set aside. You're welcome.

6. OOH, PRESENTS! I LIKE PRESENTS!!!

. . . .

OKAY, SO YOU'VE CONDITIONED yourself to make some big changes in your life. You're writing more, you're reading more, you're exercising, you're eating right. Whatever the change, you're doing it.

Now how do you maintain that change?

There are six key steps to what's known as neuro-associative conditioning that work to guarantee our new, better habits become a permanent way of life. The steps are very simple 1) decide what you really want and what's preventing you from having it now, 2) get leverage: associate massive pain to not changing now and massive pleasure to the experience of changing now, 3) interrupt the limiting pattern, 4) create a new, empowering alternative, 5) condition the new pattern until it's consistent, and 6) test it!

I want to talk today about one of the ways in which we can help instill these new behaviors until that part of our brain has grown in strength and these new, better habits are simply "the way". One of the most effective methods is reward.

Depending on the behavior we're trying to modify, the modification can be its own reward. I want to walk more. I used to walk all the time, every night after work, a good 2 hour walk, but since starting this job at the hot dog factory, I'm on my feet sometimes 10 hours a night, 6 days a week, and on my one day off, being on my feet some more is not something that appeals to me. But standing at a machine and watching hot dogs rolls by all night isn't exactly a workout. Well, sometimes, depending on how well they're running. But on average, I'm not working anything but my feet and my eyes and sometimes my hands. I feel lazy. I feel chubby. I feel I need to get off my ass and DO something. Remember, we make small changes every day that will improve our quality of life.

I also used to read a lot more than I do. So for quite a while now I've been reading a chapter a day before I ever get to work at my computer. But I usually do it on the couch in my library. Stretched out. Comfortable.

Today I put on my shorts and shoes and read my chapter while I walked. It wasn't a long walk, wasn't a far walk, just a few blocks away from my house. By the time I finished, I was sweaty, tired, and just wanted to sit down. So that was my reward. I finished the chapter and rewarded myself by coming home, kicking off my shoes, and collapsing. It was glorious.

Often I'll check my email while I'm brushing my teeth. But I don't let myself answer it until I've done that day's words. I know I could always just wait to check it until afterward, since I'm not going to answer it anyway, but this way I know there's something there waiting for me at the end, and getting to open them and reply to friends' emails is my reward for a good day's writing. Or a bad day's writing. It's my reward for TRYING some days. But it works.

For rewards like this to work, they have to be immediate. We're not going to do something difficult and reward ourselves with something later in the week. The impact is lost. Sure, we remember oh yeah I'm getting THIS because a few days ago, I did THAT. But to our brains, the connection isn't as strong as it would be if we got our reward right away. This goes back to strengthening those parts of your brain and conditioning yourself to your new habits.

Sometimes I reward myself for NOT blowing a lot of money on action figures or some other bit of geekery I don't NEED by buying myself a comic. Comics are cheaper and, to me, just as much fun.

My daughter and I are currently working our way through the new season of Mystery Science Theatre 3000 on Netflix. I would love to just take a day and watch the rest of them. But I have writing to do.

So in addition to emails I'll reward myself, especially on a day I get everything on my to-do list DONE by taking the last few hours of the day and relaxing on the couch with my sweetpea watching Jonah and the bots.

Rewards are an excellent way to convince your brain that thing you know you should do but don't want to do is really worth doing after all. What new habits are you trying to condition yourself to adopt? Write it down and then come up with a suitable reward you think would motivate you to DO it.

One warning, though, you can't use the same reward every time, otherwise you'll grow used to it and it won't serve as strongly as the reward you meant it to be anymore. Come up with several alternatives and break them up. Schedule them if you have to. God knows my love of schedules. My reward for walking tomorrow won't be sitting down. It'll probably be a shower which I'm wishing now I'd taken when I got home instead of deciding to wait until before I go to work today. Blech! I know when I've spent enough time walking that I don't feel like I'm waddling down the street anymore, my reward will be an expansion of my wardrobe once I can fit into all the old jeans I can't wear anymore but can't bring myself to throw out.

I'll get there. Sooner or later. Baby steps.

7. A CONVERSATION ABOUT DOUBT.

. . . .

"I'VE FOUND THE TIME to write every day. I've got my family on board.. But still I find it hard to sit down and DO it every day. Can you help?"

First you have to raise your standards. Stop thinking of writing as something you WANT to do every day, something you CAN do every day, and see it instead as something you MUST do every day. Even if you have to trick yourself with the reward system until you get the habit firmly established.

I knew I had a first draft I COULD finish today. But I got off work sort of late last night, didn't get a lot of sleep, and after the morning reading and walk, REALLY could have used a nap. But I had two fail safes in place for just such a day as this. One, I MUST finish this first draft. I have my weeks scheduled pretty full, working on a different project each week. Next week I start on the adaptation of a friend's movie into a novel. I've already told him I would, so I HAVE to do that next week, which means if I'm going to finish this story, it can't be next week. And with the current story, I've got three accountability partners, friends to whom I've been sending my daily word counts. I knew THEY knew I hoped to finish this story today and I'd made such a good showing of my daily words so far, I would have felt like a failure had I skipped out on today's words. So I HAD to write.

And then there was the reward aspect. I told myself if I finished this first draft today—not just added words and finished it later, but finished it TODAY—I could have Dairy Queen for lunch.

But really, these are just minor things. Because for me, I really do HAVE to write every day. MOST days, anyway. Some people exercise, some people clean, some people garden, I write. It's my drug and my safe place and the thing I spend most of my days thinking about. But if you haven't reached that point yet, you can easily use these other methods as a way to tell yourself I HAVE to do this. Get an accountability partner and think of a great reward for a job well done.

Second, change your limiting beliefs. You might be thinking I COULD write today, but I'm too tired, or I'm not inspired or I don't have any ideas or I don't have time to really dig into the meat of the story anyway so I'll just watch some YouTube videos. Believe me, I've been there, all over it, many many times.

One of the biggest hindrances we face is we're afraid it won't be any good. SO WHAT!?! It's NEVER as good in first draft as it is in final draft, so who cares if the sentences are clunky or the details aren't fleshed out or the plot is a little confusing. Christ, I wanted to write SO MANY years before I ever actually DID, but didn't because of ALL of these obstacles.

How can I possibly foreshadow something sinister later if I don't know the whole story yet? You don't! You come back later and add that detail. Do you think the first draft I just finished was perfect and beautiful from the first word all through to the end? It's 7227 words, and took five days to write. I missed a detail here and there, I messed up a plot point or dropped a bit I meant to foreshadow, I promise you. But I powered through, wrote through the doubt and finished the first draft because I know I'll just go back over it again later and fix all those broken bits and smooth out the winkles and tie up the loose ends. Writing isn't about saying it right the first time, it's just about saying it. Period. All the other stuff comes later, so whatever doubts you're carrying around in your mind as to why you have time to write but still can't, just know up front that they're bullshit.

And last, find a role model you can emulate. I don't think it takes a genius to realize my love of Stephen King. And when I heard years ago that he wrote 2000-2500 words every day, no matter how long it took at the keyboard, I knew that was the role model for me. But I was also realistic and set a realistic goal for a young writer with a day job and a family. I wrote EVERY day but I was only trying to reach 500 words. As I became more self confident and proficient at getting those 500 words, I upped it to 1000. Now, however, 26 years in I know I can do 2000 a day when I really want to. But I also know I'm not Stephen King and I do have another job to go to every night, so I'm happy to meet the 1000-1500 word goal. Even happier still if I get to 2000.

Find someone who is doing the work you want to be doing and then do what they do. Sean Combs said once that he built his empire by doing everything Russell Simmons did. Russell started a record label, Puffy started a record label. Russell started a clothing line, Puffy started a clothing line.

We need role models. Following another person's path to success is also a great way to avoid the pitfalls they faced along the way.

You have to allow yourself the ability to mess up, because making mistakes is one of the ways we learn to be better at what we do. I've messed up MANY times at my job, but never in the same way twice. It only took running out the bottom film one time to make sure I pay attention now and never do it again.

So stop being a baby, stop being afraid of that blank page. Stop seeing it as an obstacle to creating something amazing and see it instead as an OPPORTUNITY to create something amazing. The story I just finished was inspired by a very personal story a friend told me and I was terrified at first of not doing it justice. But I wrote through my doubts and now, I have to say, MAN I really really like this story. I want to say I LOVE it, but it needs another pass, it needs some smoothing out, and it needs some feedback, all of which will get done. The hard part is OVER now.

And next week I get to do it all over again with something new. And I couldn't be more excited!

8. LESSONS FROM A TWO-YEAR-OLD.

. . . .

MY YOUNGEST GRANDSON is two and that boy questions EVERYTHING. What's that? What's that? What's that? Why? Why? Why?

But that's good. We SHOULD ask questions. Questions are how we learn things, about ourselves and about the world around us. Questions have power. And the QUALITY of those questions is important, too.

I learned this lesson not too long ago. I had a lot of success with my novel THE THIRD FLOOR, so I did what any writer who'd been struggling for 20 years to make something happen and finally saw it happen would do. I tried to do it again. I dropped the writing plans I'd made and started concentrating almost exclusively on writing more Angel Hill novels. But no matter how many Angel Hill novels I wrote about ghosts, nothing hit the way THE THIRD FLOOR did. They sold, sure, they did alright. But nothing took off.

So I started asking why not. What's wrong with those books? What did I do wrong? What did I do with THE THIRD FLOOR that I didn't do with these books?

It took a while, a couple of years, in fact, before I realized the problem. I was asking the wrong questions. See, our questions determine our thoughts and I stopped seeing my writing as something I GOT to do every day and it became something I HAD to do every day. And questions have answers, so when I was asking myself what I'd done wrong the second, third, fourth times, my mind came up with answers. The books aren't good enough. You're no good at marketing. The book was a fluke and you're fated to work a crappy day job for the rest of your life and only write during your off time.

I had to change my thinking. I had to change my questions. Instead of what did I do wrong, I had remember that I'm not beholden to anyone in my writing and ask what CAN I do next? The answer was anything I want.

Instead of why did those books fail, what did I learn from writing them? I learned I CAN write a novel and not take two years to do it.

Instead of what do I need to do differently, what am I happy about in my writing? Instead of what do I regret, what am I proud of? Instead of what do I wish would change, what am I grateful for?

Once I changed my questions, my entire outlook on writing changed. I went back to all those writing plans I had years ago and decided to get back to them. Because they were good plans, and I was excited for all the things I wanted to write back then. And I'm excited again now that I'm going to write them. In fact, I've already started. I got out my calendar and scheduled the next two months, one new title a week (the one-week deadline keeps me from procrastinating and keeps me working), and now when I look ahead at what's coming up, it's always a story I'm eager to work on.

I don't know if any of these stories are going to sell. I HOPE they do, of course, but whether they do or not, I have to ask another question: since I have a day job that pays pretty well, which is more important right now, selling a lot of books, or writing a lot of books I'm excited to write? I don't even have to ponder the answer. I'm writing books I want to write again and it's changed my entire mood.

You should always ask questions, obviously. But make sure you're asking the right questions. Ask questions that are going to inspire you to move forward, NOT questions that are going to make you focus on the negative.

Questions are powerful tools, so use them wisely. The right questions can change the world. Just ask Einstein.

9. EMPOWERING WORDS EMPOWER.

. . . .

I'VE JUST HAD A BREAKTHROUGH.

I often run into people, acquaintances at work or family members I haven't seen in a while, and they'll ask me the same question every time. "You still writing those books?" And I always answer the same way. "Yep. Writing every day."

I need to stop saying that. Because words affect the way people view us. So instead, from now on when someone asks me that, I'm going to respond with, "Yeah., I'm a writer." As if to say, "DER! Did you just meet me?!?"

With any luck, that'll get it through their heads and they'll stop asking. And if they need an alternative question for the next time they see me, they can ask "Got any new books online I can buy?" That would be a much better question.

Words are such powerful things. Writers use them every day and we understand on an unconscious level what they can do. After all, we'll sit and struggle for the longest time with whether or not to use one word in favor of another. Which one better suits the emotional impact we're trying to make? Which one better conveys the horror of the situation, for horror writers. Which word choice will get the biggest laugh?

But I don't think we often stop to think about the effects our word choices can have outside of the page.

For example, I never say, "I'm going upstairs to write." Instead I say, "I'm going upstairs to work." Because I do see my writing as a job. Not just because I make some money at it, but because I treat it like a day job, a serious day job with consequences if I don't show up.

And usually this could have some negative connotations, but working doesn't bother me. As long as I enjoy the job. I could spend all day at my computer working and never give it a second thought. But even a couple of hours at night on the hot dog line and I'm constantly asking, "Are we about done yet?!?!" But again, that comes down to the words we use. I'll say, "I'm going upstairs to work," in the morning, but in the afternoon it's, "I have to go to work." The change between I AM and I HAVE TO is all the difference in the world.

(Ok, when it comes to my grandkids and I tell them I'm going upstairs and they say "Why, Pop?" I'll say, "Pops has got to go to work," but that's for their benefit, implying I don't WANT to go away, but Pops HAS to. At the same time, however, it also implies some amount of responsibility, which I'm okay with. Because the words won't write themselves.)

Sometimes, instead of, "I'm writing this story," I'll say, "I'm working on this project." Project sounds much more productive and serious. I'm writing a STORY sounds like I could do it just as easily on the couch with everyone, scribbling on a legal pad which I'm later going to shove into a drawer after everyone oohs and aahs over it for a minute. And when I do use the word "story", I try to put "work" in there with it. "I'm WORKING on a new story."

This room I'm in right now isn't "the back bedroom" or "the spare room". It is my office. I remember my very first word processor, I never called it that. Instead it was "the machine", and I did a TON of work on that thing.

It's really just a matter of finding the right euphemism, but euphemism or not, the impact of the words doesn't change. If you're struggling with finding the time, the motivation, the desire, the inspiration to sit down and write, change the words you use to talk about it. Instead of saying, "I should really sit down and get some writing done," say, "I'm going to do some work on this new project."

Instead of, "I don't have time to write," say, "I will set aside the time to write."

Instead of, "This story sucks," say, "This isn't turning out how I hoped it would. What can I do to fix it?"

As writers, we use words every single day. Now we just have to start using the RIGHT words, empowering words that will improve our emotional states and fire us up. What disempowering words do you use that could be changed?

10. READY! SET! OOH, FUNNEL CAKE!

• • • •

I'VE READ IT SEVERAL times over the years, that "writing/publishing isn't a sprint, it's a marathon." Meaning if your first book doesn't sell gangbusters right out of the gate, don't lose hope because there's plenty of time and in this new self publishing e-book world, we don't have to worry about books going out of print. So the book you wrote and published yesterday will still be able to bring you money ten years from now.

And while I believe that logic, I hate that metaphor. Writing is a marathon. God, I get winded just saying it. I have a better one.

Writing/publishing is an amusement park. Not only can you stop and rest whenever you want—there are no more contracts putting us under deadlines we might not meet—but we get to have FUN!

This monthly comic book-style series I've been writing, no one is going to buy this thing, and I know it. But I'm having a great time writing it. Every week this month I've worked on a different project, and I'll continue the practice next month because I'm really enjoying the freedom it gives me. I can spend a week on one thing, then move on and get away from that one for a while and do something different. That way, when I do get back to the previous work, I'll be able to do so with new eyes. And I won't start to resent this damn novel that just WILL NOT END!!!!!! That's something I hadn't allowed myself in a couple of years because I was stuck in that sprint/marathon mindset.

Sure, writing/publishing was a marathon, but there's only so many dollars to go around and if you don't get that new title up NOW, readers will spend their money on someone who DID hit Publish instead. So while I've got plenty of time to start making money on each particular book, I had to get those books up there as quick as I could. It may all be a marathon, but you still have to run if you don't want to be dead last to the finish line.

However, with my new weekly schedule, it's truly an amusement park. AND I feel so much more productive lately. I currently have several titles in my first draft folder. Soon I'll have several titles undergoing revision. And eventually I'll have several titles ready for publication, plus a whole new round in first draft and revision status.

For years I'd wondered how it was any writer managed to work on more than one project at a time. I never could do it. I'd always lose interest in one and drop it until the other one was finished, but with this new weekly method, I can't see why I would ever want to go back to just working on one thing at a time.

If you're a writer who wants to feel more productive and really energize your creative muscles, try this routine for two months. Get out your calendar or day planner or whatever you use and allocate the first week's writing to one project, the next week to a different project, and the week after that to something else. Do this every week for however many projects you have that you wish you had time to work on.

If you don't finish something in that week, who cares? Move on to the next one and come back to the other one next month. This week's project, adapting the script to my friend Caleb Straus's movie IT'S OVER to prose form, is not going to be even almost done this week. So I'll move on next week to something else, and come back and do some more work on this one next month. That's the thing about amusement parks, so many fun, exciting options. Why limit yourself? My daughter and I have our favorite roller coasters when we go, but we do stop and ride other things during the walk from one coaster to the other.

There's no reason at all, in this current self publishing landscape, that you should ever feel stifled or blocked. Be organized, yes, be diligent, absolutely, but also be creative. See what you can do once you allow yourself the time and space to work like a true creatively free person. I guarantee you'll be a much happier writer in the end.

What other metaphors could you replace with better, more empowering ones, to alter your emotional state when you encounter them?

11. DON'T BE AFRAID OF THE BIG BAD BLANK PAGE.

. . . .

I'VE TALKED A LOT LATELY about emotions. Well, they do control a good deal of what we do, don't they? How many times have you sat down at your desk, ready to write, only to remember something crappy that happened earlier that day, or the day before, and suddenly you find yourself blocked?

Or you've been looking forward all day to finally writing, but then you get into an argument with someone and suddenly you don't feel like it anymore. Instead you decide to go play a video game or something else you don't have to think about. Or you get some really good news and suddenly you're bouncing off the wall with energy.

One of the most overwhelming feelings we face as writers is FEAR. Fear that the work will be bad. Fear no one will like it. Fear they'll laugh at our stupidity. Fear we'll be so criticized we'll never be able to write again and then, if we can't write, what do we do with the rest of our lives?

You can overcome that fear, though. Below are six steps you can follow to master that feeling and keep it from hindering your work.

First: Identify what you're feeling. Remember, our words have power, so if you think you're afraid, you're going to be afraid. Dig in and try to dissect that feeling. Maybe it's not really fear at all. Maybe you're just anxious. Maybe it's not fear the writing won't be any good, but uncertainty because you haven't planned the story well enough yet and don't know where to go after you get that first sentence out. Maybe it's not fear everyone will hate the story, but fear that ONE PERSON will hate it. If you have one person in mind you're usually writing for—and I think most of us do—this can be a valid response. It can feel like you're letting this one person down. And in reality it's not that they won't like the story, but that they might not be as excited by it as you are. And there's nothing wrong with that.

Second: Acknowledge the feeling. Once you understand what you're really feeling, accept it. This is the best way we can insure honest communication with ourselves and the quickest way to recognize and overcome these negative feelings in the future.

Third: Inquire. Ask yourself why am I feeling this way? How do I WANT to feel? What can I do to change it? What can I learn from this situation? How have I handled it in the past?

Fourth: Be confident. This isn't your first story. Hell, chances are it's not the first story your imagined ideal reader didn't like. And, if we're being logical here, you haven't even written the thing yet, you have no idea how that person is going to react. Your fears are based on nothing more than a lack of confidence in yourself. But look at the evidence. You have how many titles already written? How many words under your belt? How many other ideas raring to go? You've done this before, many times in fact. You'll do it again many more times in the future. This project you're struggling with, once it's done, you'll wonder why it ever gave you so much trouble in the first place. It's like ripping off a band-aid. That's why you do it quickly, so the pain of the experience is over faster and you can get on with your life.

Fifth: Remember that you can handle this feeling this time and the next. Remember a time when you finished a project and handed it off to be read and the person wasn't as excited as you? Yeah, it's every time, because you're the writer and you don't see the thing the same way they do. You know all the nuances, the ones you did and didn't include. You know all the details of the work even if not all of them made it onto the page. Of COURSE their reaction isn't going to be the one you hope for. It never is. We're an ego-driven lot, we want everything we do to be brilliant and loved by all. But that's just not reality. People will like some works and not like some works quite as much. Over a decade ago, I finished a short story, "In the Town of Broken Dreams," that, when I got to the end, made me sit back with a big smile and think "Yeah, that came out just like I imagined it. First time ever. It's perfect." So I handed it off to a few first readers, and you know what? They hated it. Every single one. I mean they truly disliked this story. And I didn't get it at all. There was nothing offensive about it. It wasn't gory. I felt the writing was pretty clear and clean. But everyone who read it, none of them had any good reactions. It killed me. But, you know what? It didn't really kill me.

Instead of freaking out and giving up writing for good, I asked what about the story they didn't like. Characters, plot points, details? What was it? They all gave me great feedback and in many cases I saw they had some very good points that helped me in going back and revising certain parts of the story to make things clearer for other readers. I understood what I was feeling, why I was feeling it, and made a plan to overcome that feeling that time, and the next time—if it ever happened again. So far it hasn't. But still, some people like things, some people like things less than they like other things. So I just keep on keeping on, fighting the good fight and doing the work I was meant to do.

And finally: Take action. You've taken all the steps to overcome that pit in your stomach feeling you get when facing the blank page. You're confident. You've got a plan. Now prove it and WRITE something. Take that fear and crush it under your heel by putting down words and words and words. Write with abandon. Write with courage. Or better yet write with an absence of fear. Because in the end, what's the serious worst that can happen? If someone doesn't like something you've written, they can't kill you for it. So when it comes right down to it, no matter what someone's reaction, you're going to live to write another day. So write. And write some more. And write some more after that. And do it all again the next day.

12. GOAL!!!!!!!

• • • •

GEORGE MICHAEL SAID you gotta have faith, and while I agree with that, a fulfilling life is not built on wishes alone. You gotta have GOALS!

You have to take a minute to sit down and write out what's important to you, what things you want to achieve, what things you want to do, what things you want to own. Do you want to learn another language? Do you want to build your business into a multi-million dollar empire? Do you want to own a jet? Do you want to change the world?

For many people, yes, these are the very things they want to do with their lives. These are their goals. And some people will actually meet these goals. How? Not by sitting idly by and relying on faith, that's for sure.

So how do we achieve our goals?

Through planning and persistence.

Two years ago, I hadn't been writing much for a while. So I told myself to get back to doing the thing I love and WRITE. How to get there? I set myself the goal of publishing one new title every month for a year. But I didn't have 12 unpublished titles just sitting to the side, waiting for me to pick them up and do something with them. I did have a few already written, and that did lighten the load and make my goal that much easier to attain. But I still had a lot of work to do.

First, I told everyone what I wanted to do. Announcing your goal is a good way to get some built-in accountability, especially if you've got friends and family to support you and keep you motivated by holding you accountable. I have three or four friends that I send my word counts to every day, depending on which project I'm working on. Sometimes this is enough to keep me going, producing words, so I have something to show them. I suppose it's ego maybe? Or the need for validation? Whatever it is, it works.

Next, I made a list of all the titles I had at the ready, then figured out how many more I still needed to write.

The point of today's discussion is how to figure out those goals that will get you to where you want to be. All it takes is a few minutes. And I know what you're thinking. You've set goals before and you failed to meet them. Progress was too slow and quitting was too easy. But you're thinking about it all wrong.

Take a look at your life. Take at look at where you are. You're grown, you're reasonably responsible. Maybe you have a family. You meet goals every day. Your goal is to live, so you eat and sleep and all the other things a body needs every day to get it to the next one. Your goal is to take care of your family, so you go to a job and every week or two you get money to help pay some bills. Not every goal is met immediately. Sometimes they take time. Sometimes they take a LONG time. Look at school. The goal there is to graduate and after 13 years including kindergarten, you're there. Took forever, but one day at a time turned into one week at a time turned into one month at a time and one year at a time and before you know it, POOF! You're a high school graduate.

It's the same with any goal. So let's try something. Let's start with personal development.

Take a few minutes and write down every personal development goal you can think of. You want to write more, you want to learn more about writing, about your chosen genre, about publishing, you want to meet more writers at the same level as you, you want to meet writers more successful than you and pick their brains on how they did it. Whatever it is that you think is going to make you the writer you want to be, write it down.

Now go down that list and put a number next to each item according to how long you think that goal would take you to meet.

One year gets a 1, two years a 2, and so on. It doesn't matter if you're looking at it and wondering how you'll ever achieve this goal, we'll worry about that later. For now we're just giving ourselves a deadline. Now go through the list again and look at all those one-year goals. Which one of those do you feel is the most important at this stage of your life?

Take this goal and write down WHY you are committed to achieving this goal within the next year. How will meeting it benefit you? How will not meeting it hurt you? If the motivation is not in those answers, then reconsider either which goal IS most important, or your reasons to wanting to achieve it.

For my one title a month goal, I had, for YEARS, been the guy who makes plans and then cancels them almost at the last minute. I was pretty good at saying something SOUNDED like a good idea, but terrible at the follow through. So if I didn't meet my one title a month goal, then I was just back to being that person. And I didn't want to be that person anymore. I wanted to be someone people COULD rely on, not someone they said, "Oh, he cancelled. Again. Go figure." So for me that was a very strong motivation for doing something I said I was going to do. And I did it.

Next, career goals. Whether your business is writing, filmmaking, audio book production, or whatever, what goals would you like to achieve over the next, let's say 20 years, to get you at the top of that profession and doing only that as your day job? Write down every goal you would like to achieve.

Myself, I have an empire to build and I've already made this list and spent a LOT of last year taking the steps necessary to do it. I've got projects I spent months on last year that won't see the light of day for years more to come, but I've already begun laying the foundation so that, when the time comes, I'm already on my way.

Again, as with the personal development goals, write down next to each goal your personal timelines for achieving it. Take the most important one-year goal and write down your motivation for getting there. How will this goal benefit you? How will not meeting it hurt you? Etc.

Let's have some fun. Let's look at some play goals.

Personally, I want to build my comic book collection. I want to collect the first appearances of all the major Marvel and DC Comics characters. I've got a good start so far, both mining my pre-existing collection and buying some pretty cool back issues online. It's gonna take a while to achieve this goal, but it's important enough to me and I've already got a plan for getting there, over time. This isn't a one-year goal, mind you, but I know it's going to take some time so I've already got started on it.

What fun and exciting things do you want to do with your life? Want to travel? Take your family on a nice vacation? Buy a pool? Want to get the entire collection of Prince and Bowie albums on vinyl? (me too!!!)

Follow the same steps as before.

Last, what some call contribution goals and I call pay it forward goals. Do you want to help an at-risk child? Build an animal shelter? Feed the hungry? Adopt a family for Christmas?

Again, follow those same steps, picking the most important of those goals that you can accomplish within the next year, write down WHY it's important to you.

The next step, some would say one of the most important steps, is GETTING STARTED. No, you don't have to take a big, major step right now in accomplishing your goal, but you must do SOMETHING. If your goal is to have a novel written within the next 12 months, come up with a title. Name your main characters. If your goal is to spend the next week off work cleaning your house, start with the upstairs bathroom. Okay, that was my goal and that was the step I took today. I'm not finished, but I took the first step in meeting my goal for this week. Later today I'll take another step. Tomorrow I'll take another. The day after, I'll take another.

No matter how big or small that first step, as soon as you decide on your goal, TAKE A STEP toward achieving it. A goal with no forward momentum is disposable, forgettable, and will ultimately be a failure.

So you're probably wondering about all those other goals you wrote down. The 2-year, 5-year, 10-year, 20-year goals. You'll get to those. This first one-year goal is just to show you how easily goals CAN be achieved when you take them one step at a time and do what's necessary to make them happen. Once you've made some progress on the first goal and seen just how easy it really is, you'll have gained the confidence and experience necessary to start meeting ALL of your goals every time.

I know not everything I want to do with my life is going to just fall into my lap, so I have to make a plan, EXECUTE the plan, and follow through. You're feeling like life is kicking you in the ass, and sometimes it does. But we work through it, we raise our standards for what we will and won't accept in our lives, and we start living the movie we've always seen in our heads, one step at a time, one goal at a time.

1Also, a very important final note: once you've met one of your goals, always have another goal right there, ready to go. As soon as I made those 12 titles in a year happen, I was ready to go on the next year's goals. The reason so many people die soon after retiring (I used to listen to these stories all the time at my last job; no one had retired from that place and lived more than a couple of years—one guy died on the way home from his retirement party!) is because people need something to look forward to. Even if you're living one Marvel Cinematic movie at a time, you've got something to keep you going. Meet your goals, but always have the next one waiting and ready to go as soon as you meet the first one.

13. PERCEPTIONS AND HOW WE DEAL WITH THEM

• • • •

I'VE BEEN THINKING a LOT lately about writer's block. Not just the act of sitting there staring at your computer, unable to type words onto the page. I mean the real gut-wrenching sort of writer's block that keeps a writer from even sitting at their computer in the first place. And this got me to thinking about perceptions and how we deal with things mentally.

Sometimes we can feel hindered by something so simple as a change of surroundings or a change of the tools we use. When I moved from writing longhand to writing directly from the keyboard, I had a tough time. I wasn't used to it and I thought I'd never get the hang of it. Same thing when I moved from a word processor to a computer. I don't know why this change gave me so much trouble. Or rather, I didn't know at the time. And then, when my son got older and I gave up my old office so he and his brother wouldn't have to share a room anymore, and I moved my stuff downstairs, the new surroundings messed with me at first.

Eventually I got the hang of all of these changes and got to a point where I can write in any room, on any machine, at any time of day. And that's because I learned to get control of my perceptions when it came to writing.

See, we're simple, stupid creatures, and we get an idea or a rhythm in our heads and from that moment on that's just the way things are. We have a really good day at work, so we try to replicate everything we did that morning, down to driving the exact same route and trying to park in the exact same spot. And then when we do all the right rituals and STILL have a bad day at work, we get upset and wonder what went wrong and it throws us into a tailspin.

Ok, maybe not US, but definitely ME. So I stopped taking the old "good luck" route to work and now just try to take the shortest. And I don't insist I can only write in THIS room, in THIS chair, at THIS desk, on THIS device. Because I know it's all a load of crap.

To get out of those defeatist mindsets and into more empowering ones, we first have to determine our emotional state when coming to these "conclusions". If I'm having a bad day already and then have to go to work and have another bad night, I'm going to blame the route I took, the jeans I wore, the order in which I got dressed then packed my lunch vs. packed my lunch and then got dressed. If I'm having a good day and have a good night at work, I'm going to do the same thing, evaluate every move I made that day, trying to replicate the good day. When really it all depends on the mood I was in. If I was in a bad mood and had a bad night, or was in a good mood and had a bad night, or vice versa on ANY of those conditions, it's going to affect how I see my preparation ritual when, in reality, what I wore or what route I took to get there has NOTHING to do with any of that. And the same thing applies to writing.

You want to write, but you're having a rough day and you're afraid that writing in that mood is going to turn out terrible work. So you avoid it. Or the last time you had a bad writing day, you were in a great mood all day, and you're in a great mood now, and that's got you paranoid about trying to write. Again, the conditions really have nothing to do with the writing, it's all your own confused perceptions. You have to get out of that mindset by...

Asking yourself the RIGHT questions. You want to write, but you ask yourself "What if I try and nothing comes out?" Or "What if I try and it turns out terrible and I have to delete it? I've just wasted a day." How about instead you think about a time when what you wrote was beautiful, exciting, detailed and moving. Ask yourself, "What if I try to write and it turns out amazing?" Or "What if I sit down just intending to get a quick hundred words out and instead write 1500?"

Your thoughts are going to be affected by the questions you ask yourself, as the questions lead your mind down one thought process or another. You can ask yourself negative questions and turn away from the computer, defeated before you even try, or you can ask empowering questions and psych yourself up to have one of your best writing days ever.

What do you believe? Do you believe that, if you have a rough writing day that you're just wasting your time, time you could have spent with your family? Or do you believe that if you have a rough writing day that at least now you know what NOT to write when you sit down the next day? Do you believe that, if you finish this project to the best of your ability and it does well when it's published, you'll be able to take some time off from the day job and get that family time you wanted? Do you believe that this project, this short story, this novella, this novel, this series, is going to touch at least one life in some significant way? Because it will. But only if you *write it*.

Our beliefs determine our expectations determine our actions. If you believe the project you're working on is important, you'll begin to expect yourself to put in the work. But if you believe the project you're working on is going to have no affect, is going to sit there, unread like all the others, then sooner rather than later, the effort you put into it is going to peter off. You MAY finish it, but you probably won't. And if you do, it's going to be lackluster work because you expect lackluster results.

Stop hindering yourself with negativity at every turn.

Last, check your references. We filter everything through the lifetime of built-up reference material in our brains. You wrote that one story that turned out terrible and everyone hated it, so why bother writing this one? You published that one book that sold gangbusters, so let's write another, similar book in hopes of a second lightning strike. You sat there for two hours that time and only managed 250 new words. Or you spent an hour at your desk that one day and wrote 2000 words!

We take these past experiences and let them affect our future performance because, for us, these are the only references we have. And oftentimes we focus on the negative ones. Which really confuses me because, growing up, I KNOW I had more disappointing Christmases than I did great Christmases. You know how I know this? Because I only remember the great ones. And I don't remember a lot of Christmases. Growing up, until I was 13 it was mostly just my mother and I, so most of my childhood memories it's just the two of us. But in all those 13 years, the days I remember most clearly were the good days. The day my mother took me to the carnival as a surprise and we were the only two there riding the Scrambler over and over. I remember many trips to see horror movies. I remember comics picked up at the grocery store while doing the shopping. I remember a bike for my birthday one year. Know what I don't remember? The off days. The days we just sat around watching television.

My mind recalls with great clarity those good days and so few of the others I'm not even sure they really happened. But it's so easy for my mind to remember all the days I sat at my keyboard and didn't add a single word to my then-current project. Or it remembers all of the rejections, but only the first few acceptances.

And if your mind works the same way, and I'd be willing to bet it does, then YOUR references are going to draw from the negative experiences more often, too. You have to train yourself to think in the opposite direction.

You have finished writing projects before, so why is this one giving you hassle? Because there were writing projects before that gave you hassle. But remember, you broke through those barriers and you finished them. You made a plan, you broke the story, got it clear in your muddled head, and you wrote the thing.

And some of those stories succeeded while some of them failed, but you didn't dwell on that because you're a writer and writing is what you do. You don't think about what comes after. You don't think about sales or reviews. Those are reference points that only came into your sphere of influence later, after years at the keyboard, years of rejections, before you ever got that first acceptance, that first publication. You wrote long before you ever had the chance for a bad review, or a month with no sales. In fact, I'd be willing to bet there was a time when you would have gladly taken a bad review or a whole month where you didn't sell a single title, as long as it meant your work was OUT THERE.

See, because back then you didn't have those reference points. Your only reference point back then was the joy and satisfaction that came from typing THE END after several days of excellent work at the keyboard.

And THOSE are the points to focus on. They're the only ones that matter. The way we motivate ourselves to move forward is by seeing the progress we're making, so if your view of the world is only showing you the struggle, shift your gaze and see the words piling up one at a time until there's a sentence, a paragraph, a page.

Our "reference library" grows every day. There's always a new opportunity for growth, a new chance to ask yourself the RIGHT questions. Every day you sit down at that page, you're empowering yourself to fight past the negative by turning your back on it and focusing on the good things. The fire in your heart when you reach the end, the feeling of accomplishment when you can hold the finished product in your hands. Or just the knowledge that today you had a choice, WRITE or DON'T WRITE, and you looked at where you are in life, then looked at where you want to be, and you made the right decision.

14. "CLEVER PUN ABOUT VALUES"

• • • •

I WAS READING TODAY about values and looking at the examples given. Things like Love, Success, Freedom, Intimacy, Security, things like that. And the book was talking about putting your values into a hierarchy to determine what in life is most important to you. So I went down the list and tried my best to order the ten examples given, and I wound up deleting two of them, and combining a couple of others. When I got done, I realized all the values listed could be narrowed further and put into one of two categories, Love or Money, with Health being a separate value all its own. Well, yeah, Love and Money are important. Which is more important? Meh, depends on the day, I guess.

But at the end of the day, what I discovered about myself is that a lot of the things listed in this book just weren't that important to me. Adventure? Nah. Power? Meh. Freedom? Well...

So I did my usual thing and decided to adapt this lesson about values and gear it toward writing. And these are the ten values I came up with:

Productivity
Quality
Consistency
Originality
Presentation
Sales/Marketing
Pioneering
Community
Coaching
Balance

Then I put them in order of most important to least. And here's what I got:

1) Productivity

2) Quality

3) Consistency

Actually, all three of these could tie for first place because each one is a cornerstone of building a writing career. We have to produce quality work consistently. These are the values that drive my day, EVERY day and they're why I'm able, even if I pulled a 12-hour shift the night before and have had a whopping four hours of sleep, to get up and sit myself down at my computer and do SOMETHING writing-related that day.

4) Balance

As writers, we could easily spend every waking hour in front of the computer, working on a draft, editing, cover design, book layout, marketing ideas, reading other writers' blogs, whatever. As long as it's writing-related, we're in every second we're conscious. But many of us have families, and the only way to maintain that family is to find a healthy work/family balance. I find the best way to do this is to focus on writing when everyone else is either asleep or not home. For over a decade I was up at 4:00 every morning, writing for two hours before work. Now that I work nights and my wife works days, I'm writing in the morning, spend time with my kids and/or grandkids in the afternoon before work. I get the work done and still have time for my family.

5) Originality

6) Pioneering

Who wants to churn out derivative work? Originality is so very important in establishing yourself and building that audience. Sure, people gravitate towards the familiar, but if you're just re-writing early King novels, how far can you get, really?

Also, it doesn't hurt to have a bit of a pioneer spirit. I'm not even going to tell you the number of ideas I've had over the years that I didn't move on and that eventually became the norm. Hell, in 2000 I had the idea to publish short stories myself in chapbook form and sell them on my website directly to readers. Another writer/editor/publisher told me that would be a huge mistake, so I forgot it. Ten years later, self-publishing is in and a few years after that, it's the norm. Publishing short stories and selling them directly to readers without an agent or some other middleman? Who'd have thunk it???

Grumble...

I had another idea about five years ago, when Kindle publishing was just picking up steam, to get some friends and publish a regular monthly or quarterly SERIAL publication with installments every issue telling a longer story. I didn't move on it and less than a year later, serials are all the rage.

Aw, COME ON!!!

If you've got that next big idea that sets your world on fire and you're not seeing anyone else out there doing it, get off your dead ass and DO IT. Be the pioneer everyone else wants to copy. This is why some of my true writing heroes are musicians like Prince, Bowie, and Trent Reznor. They wrote their way into history by consistently turning out quality work and blazing new trails people had never associated with music before. THAT'S how you win at life.

7) Coaching

I'm not saying I'm a MASTER at this thing just yet, this writing and publishing thing we do, but I've been at it a long time, over half my life, and while I don't know everything, I know a lot. And if I can help some younger authors skip some of the mistakes I made, bypass a few roadblocks before they get to them, or just find the inspiration that's all around them a lot easier, how can I not want to help? There's room on the "shelves" for everybody, and if your work is of a consistently high quality, people are going to want to read it, so why be stingy?

I've picked up a lot of tips over my currently 26 years of writing, and I'm more than happy to share and help in any way I can.

8) Presentation

I suppose maybe this one should be higher on my list, especially in the self-publishing world. But then I think of all the books I've read and how I've never once put a book down and refused to read it because it wasn't presented in the prettiest package.

I think what readers really want is an entertaining story. And that's what I do my damnedest to provide. If I put the copyright and dedication stuff at the front of the book or the back, if I have a call to action or not, if I forget to ask readers to leave a review, it's not the end of the world. The book will still, hopefully, speak for itself. The STORY is what's important, not whether my page numbers are at the top or the bottom of the page.

9) Community

Remember that author/editor/publisher who told me not to self publish short stories and sell them directly? The alternative advice he then gave me was to join some horror writer message boards, so that's what I did and I met some AMAZING people. You ask me, you will never find a more caring, accepting, cooperative group of people than horror writers. Maybe it's because we get all our negativity out on the page and have nothing but positivity left over for real life people. Maybe it's because we know making a living as a "horror writer" is tough enough without adding being an asshole to everyone you meet to it. Whatever the reason, a sense of community in such a lonely field as writing is very important. Now, it only shows up at #9 on MY list, but I was never great at meeting new people anyway. And I do currently have a pretty tight-knit group of friends I refer to as Team Flash. They've got my back and I've got theirs, all day every day. This one may be higher on your list.

10) Sales/Marketing

Again, another one that should be higher on my list, especially if I ever intend to make a real living and quit that damned day job. But, I'm just not good at it. I try like hell sometimes, but every so often it just feels like, no matter what I do, nothing has any affect, and any sale I get is just good luck and happenstance. I am working on becoming better at it, though. I've read a couple of sales books and am trying to figure out how to apply what I read there to marketing and selling books. It's not the same animal at all in most cases, but I think a good deal of the general principles can be applied.

So there you have it, my value hierarchy. As I grow as a person and as a writer, I expect some of these items may take different places on the list. Some may fall off completely and other, different, values may take their place. I'd definitely like to see coaching take a higher place on the list. But for now, this is where I stand and where I direct my energy every day.

What are some of your values and where do they fall in your value hierarchy?

15. "IT IS NOT WISE TO VIOLATE THE RULES UNTIL YOU KNOW HOW TO OBSERVE THEM."—T.S. ELIOT

• • • •

RULES, MAN. IF THEY'RE good enough for your kids, they're good enough for you. And, as with your kids, rules are only as effective as your commitment to them.

You ever get up on a Saturday morning, get your coffee, and head immediately to your office to write, only to get halfway there and your spouse or your kids come to you with a list of other things they need you to do first? Or worse, INSTEAD?

That's because while you know what you wanted to do with your morning, they don't know, and unless you communicate it to them, they're not going to know, and they're not going to care. They don't know your rules.

When my wife and I got together, she knew I loved to write. She knew I wanted to write. What she didn't know was I HAVE to write. She was ... 17? at the time. I was 19. And I hadn't made it clear yet that writing wasn't an option in my life, but a necessity. Once that became clear to her, I stopped having to bargain for time alone at my desk to get down a hundred words or so every few days. Once I'd made it clear writing consistently was a RULE, it stopped being an issue and just became "the way".

But if I hadn't shown her how serious my commitment was, she probably never would have clued in. Because her rules differed from mine. To her writing wasn't a paying job, so it couldn't be anything more than a hobby, and no one needs to work at their hobby EVERY DAY. Whereas I had an entirely different perspective. Writing wasn't my JOB—yet—but I knew if I one day wanted to make it my job, I had to, as Michael Dean of PodcastJuice.net likes to say, "work it like a job." And anyway, writing was my Zen. When all the pressures of being young and broke started to get to me, I could shut it off for an hour, make up a story that, hopefully would sell for a few bucks, and then come back to regular life with a clear head.

There are people in your life who are going to push back when it comes to the thing you love to do, because they have a different set of rules than you do. This is going to cause some arguments, I guarantee it. And the only way to get them on board is to COMMUNICATE with them just what exactly are your rules. And since they clearly have a different set of rules than you, you need to learn their rules at the same time. Only with a clear understanding of where the other person is coming from can we really find that middle ground that works for everyone. And the only way to do THAT is if YOU know your rules.

I sat down today and came up with a list of the ten most important rules I live my writing life by every single day. A few of these rules concern the other people in my house, and after 20+ years, they know them very well. The rest are strictly for my own benefit to make sure I live my writing life by a certain standard and that I NEVER dip below that.

My writing rules for life are, in no particular order:

1) Finish what you start.

2) Respect the process

3) Respect the craft.

4) Always do my best.

5) Only write what I'm in love with.

6) Make time at least 6 days a week to write. (1 hour at least, but 2 is better)

7) Always have something going, never be "between projects".

8) Follow the editing process.

9) Make marketing a regular part of the process.

10) Never get so wrapped up in work that regular life begins to suffer.

What are some of your rules for your writing life, and how committed are you to living by them every day?

16. SHAPES OF THINGS AND REFERENCES.

• • • •

I HAVE READ THAT "IT'S the moments of our lives that shape us." And that is true.

Have you ever considered how you got to this point in your life? What decisions had to be made, what people had to influence you? I think about it all the time. Because life really is just a series of choices, and we don't always make the right ones.

I also spend a lot of time thinking about fate. Was I going to wind up here on this day, in this place, doing this thing, no matter what decisions I made? I like to think NO, that I have some say in the matter. But then I also take great comfort at times knowing that "the universe is right on schedule" and things are unfolding as they're meant to unfold. But those are totally competing ideas, so I'm still working on that.

The choices I'm going to make will be influenced by the choices I've already made. If I'm smart, I'll avoid making choices that will lead to pain based on past experiences of pain, and I'll continue to make choices that give me pleasure based on similar pleasurable decisions in the past. But what were those decisions that led me here? Where am I?

I'm a writer. I'm a horror writer. I'm a horror writer who writes almost every day (depending on my schedule, sometimes I'll skip Saturday, but that's it). I'm a horror writer who, over 26 years in this business, has gained a lot of friends who are also writers, but not all of them are horror writers. I'm a writer who takes great pleasure in self-publishing and the control it gives me over the finished product.

How did I get here? I could fill a 100,000 word book giving a detailed account of all the people and events that have shaped me over 44 years. But I won't. I will, however, give credit to a few of the most important ones. When I look back at who and what led me to this day, in this place, doing this thing, I think of...

The Exorcist is my earliest memory and I've been a die-hard horror fan ever since.

Lisa Jackson was a babysitter when I was in grade school. She was in high school and she used to have to write stories for one of her classes. This lit a spark in a very young me.

Mike Swope is a friend I worked with in the early 1990s. He was also a writer who published his own chapbooks. I was fascinated by the process and the outcome. This gave me encouragement that I too could write.

Christina Schellhorn was a local writer who wanted to make writer friends, so she started the St. Joseph Literary Guild. I later became president of the Guild and wrote and published its monthly newsletter. This gave me confidence to speak and write like a professional, to conduct myself as if I knew what I was doing even when I didn't.

Dave Barnett was my first professional acceptance. And years later during an email exchange he remembered the story. I started copy editing for his Necro Publications and gained invaluable insight into horror and publishing. He's also the one who suggested I get on some message boards and meet people.

Stephen King's THE CYCLE OF THE WEREWOLF was the first book I read cover to cover in one sitting. It gave me a taste for story as a whole thing.

Stephen King's THE DARK HALF was the book that made me a reader. I'd read many books before, but always one at a time, here and there whenever one struck my fancy. But reading THE DARK HALF, I not only got inspired to stop thinking about writing but actually WRITE. I also never stopped reading after that and I've always got a book I'm reading now.

Scott Meade was my best friend all through high school. We were walking home together one day and we stopped at a drug store so he could pick up some comics. I grabbed one while I was at it. I'd always liked comics but never really collected any on a consistent basis. That all changed that day. Now I can't imagine my life without comics, they're such a huge part of who I am.

David Bain. I met Dave over a decade ago when he edited an anthology I submitted to, then edited a short story collection I enjoyed. I invited him to an anthology I was editing, and a couple years after that we started exchanging music on a daily basis. We swap war stories, ideas, good news and bad. He's one of the best writers I know and he continually inspires me to keep going.

I've made a lot of bad decisions where writing and publishing are concerned, but they were my decisions and I live with them. I'll use those references of the past, both good and bad, to continue guiding myself along this path, hopefully to even better, more productive and successful places.

What references do you have that you use to draw on in helping you decide what move to make next? What events from your past have shaped you?

Take a minute to write down the five most important or memorable references and how they have positively shaped your life. Now, write down some possible FUTURE references you'd like to be able to draw on. Find someone you admire and see how they got to where they are and maybe use THEM as your reference—who said you could only learn from YOUR mistakes?

Another big reference for me is Prince. I admired not only his ability to write, produce, perform his own music, but his insistence on it. NO ONE was going to tell him how to build his career, but him. Even as a 19-yer-old kid with no experience, he believed enough in himself and his art that he would be the only one to touch it. I can't tell you what a huge influence that has always had on me.

Bowie was another huge reference for me. I read in one book or another that during one of his mid-70s tours, he had numerous records sold, was touring constantly, was a huge star, but still had to borrow money from his manager for cigarettes. That was the turning point where Bowie took over the reigns of his own career and ascended to even newer heights, eventually becoming one of, if not THE, British rock start with the highest net worth. I used to wonder what that must be like for his kids, knowing there's not another British musician in the world worth more money than your dad. That's got to mess with your head. That's also got to build some amazing reference points for those kids.

How could I not mention Trent Reznor? Like Prince, he wrote and performed all the music on his albums, using a band only for touring purposes. These people just keep on proving that one artist can make a HUGE difference in the world, one artist can change the course of a trend with nothing more than a good idea and the commitment to bringing it to fruition.

How can I be committed to anything less?

And I believe I can achieve those levels I seek by using my references, calling upon my memories and experiences, as well as the experiences of people who've been where I want to be.

It's got me very excited for the future.

• • • •

THIS MORNING ON MY walk I was reading about identity, how we view ourselves and how others view us. And I started questioning things. How do I view myself? What is my identity?

I'm a husband, a father, a grandfather, a child, and a writer. These are the terms by which I define myself every day. Yes, I have a day job, but I never identify myself as a machine operator because I never wake up in the morning or look in the mirror and think "machine operator." That's something I DO, but it's most definitely not something I AM.

So why do I view my identity as those other things? Because that's who I am. I am a husband, a father to three children, a grandfather to two, a child to my parents, and I am a writer.

Now, those other things are genetic—in the case of husband, legal—so I'm those things whether I want to be or not. Luckily, I want to be. As for writer ... no one made me be a writer. No one asked me to be. No one suggested I be. I'm a writer because I write.

I've heard people ask several times over the years, "Is it okay to call yourself a writer when you've never published anything?" Hell yes. Once you've published, you become a "published author". I called myself a writer long before I ever published anything. Because I wrote. I wrote every day. But ... I didn't call myself a writer in the beginning.

Because I wasn't a writer, not yet. I was a guy who had written, or was writing something at the time. But I wasn't a ... WRITER.

When did I become a writer? When I started thinking of myself as a writer.

I started my writing journey with a story called THE MAN IN THE WINDOW, a little idea that had been plaguing me for a while until I finally sat down and WROTE it. But I wasn't a writer, not yet. I then wrote a very short piece for school. I still wasn't a WRITER. I was a guy who had written and was writing something at the time.

But then I wrote another story. And I wrote another. And there was one after that. Soon writing was all I thought about. My entire day centered around when would I get some time alone to write? What would I work on? Where was the story going? What would I work on next?

I was a writer. Why? Because I stopped thinking of myself as a guy who had written or was writing something at the time, and started thinking of myself as a Writer. And once I started seeing myself as a writer, others did, too. And once they started seeing me as a writer, their behavior toward me changed.

To acquaintances I was no longer the quiet guy with his nose in a book all the time, I was the writer who was busy working something out in my head. To family I was no longer the loner who spent all his time in his room and never wanted to socialize, I was the writer who was probably hard at work on his next masterpiece. And with my wife and kids, once that association clicked in their heads, I was no longer dad or husband who would rather go off by himself for a couple hours every day instead of spending time with them. Instead I was dad who had to get a little work done in his office and we'd do something as soon as that was done.

I'm telling you, how people treat you is based on how they view you, and how they view you is based LARGELY on how you view yourself.

Remember a few chapters ago when I said I used to always be the guy who made plans and then cancelled at the last minute? It got so bad, friends stopped being surprised when I would do it. It was probably expected. But I saw myself as that guy, too, and I hated it. So I decided that wasn't me. That's who I USED to be. Who am I now? The guy who says he's in and follows through. Sure, there are times I don't want to, times I've got very little free time as it is and would rather relax and recharge in my off hours from the day job. But I said I would and, let's face it, doing so isn't going to kill me. So I get off my lazy ass and do what I said I would whether it's give somebody a ride or ... well, whatever. If I said I would, I do it.. And guess what, none of it's killed me yet. The world spins and the sun sets and everything is just fine. And the more times I follow through when I made plans, the more confident I feel in myself and then that's more confidence others will have in me. And before long, I'm NOT that guy anymore. That becomes who I USED to be.

A change in MY thinking leads to a change in THEIR thinking about ME.

So, writing and being a writer.

My friends and family don't see me as a writer because I tell them I'm a writer. They see me as a writer because I write. I consistently get to my desk at least 6 days a week and I write. I may take a day here to work on some covers. Or I may take a week there to write reviews. But I'm writing. I finish and publish the projects I start. I'm organized. I'm committed. Whether I sell anything or not, whether I'm famous or not, is not the point. I'm a Writer, so I write.

And all it takes is deciding that's who you want to be, and then BEING that. There were times early on, before I identified myself as a "writer", when I'd skip a day or two, maybe three, maybe I'd put aside whatever I was working on and come back to it some other time. Because I wasn't a writer, I was just a guy who had written or was writing something at the time. So big deal if I blow it off for a few days. It's not like I'm a WRITER. I'll get to it when I get to it.

But you know what? I sometimes never got to it. How many stories did I let die because I set them aside and just never picked them up again? I have a file stuffed full of half-finished projects. But then I made that switch and stopped being THAT guy and started being a WRITER, and I started finishing things. I wasn't the fastest writer in the world, but I was committed and I finished things. I wasn't the

BEST writer in the world, but I was committed and I got better. I wasn't the most popular writer in the world, but I was committed and I gained readers who turned into fans who turned into friends. And now I know I have people ready to read whatever I write and, I gotta say, that drives me along every day, too. I want to finish THIS story because I know there will be people eager to read it. I want to finish THAT book because I want to show my appreciation for the people who buy my books and spend their valuable time reading them.

I'm a writer, man. This is what I do. Hell, I can't imagine a life where I'm not a writer. Even if self publishing goes away and I never again make another sale or publish another book, I'm going to write. Because I'm a writer. Try and stop me. I fucking dare you.

Now, who are YOU? Better yet, who do you WANT to be? Good. Now forget your past and go make it happen.

18. WHAT, ARE YOU GONNA CRY ABOUT IT?

• • • •

THIS MAY SEEM LIKE a strange topic today, but hear me out.

I have a friend who once said he imagined that, at the end of the world, I would be on a mountaintop eating Twinkies and watching the world burn. He said this because I am, on average, a blank. It's not that I have no emotions, but I hold them in check. I used to have a temper. My old bedroom wall at my mother's house—made famous as the room where Milo Dengler arranged the bodies of his murdered children in THE THIRD FLOOR—had cracks and holes in the walls from where I'd punched them. But that's no way to live.

So I had to do something about that. For me, it seemed pretty simple. I made two realizations. 1) NOTHING in life is worth getting THAT upset over, and in five years whatever the big deal was today isn't going to mean a damn thing. And 2) people look really friggin' stupid when they're grown adults throwing temper tantrums.

So whenever I feel myself getting pissed or even just slightly upset I remember these two things and it helps me to face the problem with a blank face. It's not that I'm dead inside—my kids can tell you that—I just think it's much easier to face my problems with my HEAD instead of my heart.

But how can you master your emotions, and how the hell does this apply to writing?

First thing's first. You have to understand your emotions and label them. What emotions do you run through in a typical week? Happy? Sad? Angry? Loved? Anxious? Disappointed? I think most emotions are just varying degrees of these few. Happy gives way to thrilled gives way to ecstatic while angry stems from frustrated and gives way to furious. The first step in mastering something is naming it. So these are our main emotions we deal with in a given week. You may have others, emotions specific to the life you live.

Now let's look at the negative ones and make a list of the things in our lives that trigger these emotions. Unexpectedly, and unnecessarily, long nights at work for me. Or getting there and finding out first shift did only a small fraction of the schedule leaving second shift to finish it. I can feel myself getting heated just typing those sentences. What else? You know what? I think that's about it, honestly. In any given day, the only things that really bother me are work-related, and mostly because of the nature of my job and the company I work for.

But I don't spend all night in a pissy mood. Why not? Because I moved on to the next step, which was finding something that could trigger the opposite reaction. Being pissed off all night isn't going change anything, and in fact it's just going to make the night even worse. So I changed my thoughts, which changed my emotions. I employ this technique CONSTANTLY at work.

I ask myself new questions. Not why did first shift only get three out of twelve blends done? Instead, I ask how am I going to decide on my main character's name? What is his job, and does that job affect the plot or vice versa, or is it just a job he happens to have? Instead of focusing on the fact it's going to be another 10 hour night while first shift got to leave on time, I focus on a solution instead of the problem. Write. Write a killer short story, write a killer novella, write a killer novel that sells well enough I can take a lesser paying job where I have more time and energy. Better yet, write something that sells so well I don't have to work a day job anymore. And then I can write MORE books.

See, I've had plenty of nights where I felt completely trapped by life. "I can't accept that THIS is how the course of my life will go from now on." Good, because it's not. This isn't my first job. Most likely it won't be my last. And unlike a LOT of the people I work with, I have something to get me out of my head and to give me hope to work toward. I'm a writer. And writing doesn't have an expiration date. Well, it does, but that'll be the day I die. I can work at this every day for the rest of my life and no one can stop me. So that means, no matter how bad my day job ever gets, I've always got this backup plan. And I'm not sleeping on the backup plan, I'm working at it 6 days a week, with the faith that THIS is not my life. It's just my life RIGHT NOW. And that fills me with hope, happiness, and, believe it or not, sometimes with love for all things because in those moments, God smiles on me.

But it's the same for every negative feeling I have. I know that, whatever it is, it's just right now. In five years, who's going to care? Who's even going to remember?

Letting your emotions control you is a sure path to failure. Your emotions, like anything else that affects your life, are only meant to act as a periphery. Just like logic needs the balance of emotions, emotions also need to be tempered with logic.

So the next time you feel the walls closing in and you start to get anxious or frustrated or pissed off, think of your art. The films you plan to make, the music you plan to record, the painting you plan to do, or the fiction you plan to write. Stop focusing on the thing that's causing all the negativity and put your head into that place where you get to be free. And then remember this thing, this pain, is not forever. Soon you'll be away from it and back where you want to be, behind the camera, in front of the easel, or at the keyboard.

At least, that's what works for me...

19. GET OFF YOUR DEAD ASS BEFORE YOUR ASS IS DEAD.

• • • •

THERE ARE A COUPLE of serious dangers writers face. There's Carpal Tunnel, eye strain, backaches, overeating (who doesn't have a little something handy when they're writing?). When your job consists of sitting at a desk and typing all day, and there's not a regular clocking out time, no regularly scheduled lunches or even days off, you're facing a lot health risks.

For a long time, I kept trying to counter this lifestyle by working out in the mornings before I went to my office. I never felt healthier, never felt more energetic. In fact, I often found I needed a nap around mid-afternoon. And I don't mean a nap would hit the spot, I mean I NEEDED a nap.

I know a lot of writers counter this by buying a standing desk, but I stand all night at my other job, and anyway I just spent a couple hundred on the desk I bought 3 years ago. I'm NOT buying another desk.

So lately I've gotten back into doing something I used to do before I got this job, when I actually had time off work every week. When I get up in the morning, before I've done ANYTHING, even before I turn on my computer, I grab a book and take a walk. I used to have a route I walked every day, and it took about 2-2 ½ hours. I don't take that route anymore because now I'm just walking while I read another chapter. Sometimes it's 30 minutes, sometimes it's an hour. And I like to change it up and take a different route every day now just to keep it interesting.

And I have to say, having been back out there doing it for a few weeks now, the benefits are amazing.

I got to bed last night around 1:30. I got up today at 7:30. While six hours of sleep is very common for me, that doesn't mean I don't get tired during the day. Hell, I'm tired all the time, actually. But even when I get to bed later and only manage about five hours of sleep, I haven't been hitting that I HAVE TO LAY DOWN wall lately. I attribute it to walking. Well, that and drinking a lot more water with lemon. That's what I take to work now instead of Sierra Mist or something.

But back to the walking. The problem with all the working out I was doing before was, while it's GOOD to work out, I don't think it was the right kind of exercise for me. You should be able to carry on a conversation, your breathing should be audible but not labored. But working out I wasn't breathing right, I certainly wasn't stretching nor did I allow myself a winding down period, which is important.

It's really the difference between an aerobic workout and an anaerobic workout. An anaerobic workout is something like lifting weights or sprinting, anything that requires a "short exertion, high-intensity movement". It works your body, but your burning sugar, not fat. You can get FIT without getting HEALTHY. Jim Fixx was FIT but not necessarily HEALTHY. We want to be HEALTHY. And we're writers, we don't need bulging muscles, we just need to keep that sitting-around weight off. And aerobic exercise not only burns fat, but also prevents clogged arteries which can prevent heart disease.

Sure, standing is better for you than sitting, but how much aerobic exercise are you getting there, REALLY?

Take a break. Take a book, or an audio book, or a pod cast, and LEAVE YOUR HOUSE for a change.

We're solitary inside creatures, that's our nature, but there's a world outside and the sun is shining and the flowers are blooming and while the air may not be perfect out there, I guarantee it's less stale than in your stuffy old office.

Something else I like about walking. It's addictive. Some days I hope for a long chapter, because I just want to enjoy being out there.

And I know I could just keep walking longer if I wanted to, but I use the chapter a day method to keep my focus and make sure I come back and get to work on that day's writing. Otherwise, I'd be out there all day and have nothing left when I get to work that night. But it's definitely something I look forward to every morning now.

I admit walking might not be your thing. But for God's sake, do SOMETHING. It's so easy to fall into the trap of sitting down at work all day, then coming home and sitting down at home night, but what would you rather do, get off your ass and do something for an hour a day and have many more days to do them, or do nothing and have fewer days left? I don't know about you, but I'm hoping to live as long as humanly possible, so I'm getting up and moving, getting my heart rate up and letting the blood flow, breathing, and getting some sun on my face.

I feel I definitely have more energy, my mood's a lot better, and if I do say so myself, I'm doing some pretty damn good work on the page lately too.

It's not ALL from walking. Like I said, lemon water instead of whatever else you were drinking. The benefits there alone are awesome. And also when I get home from my walk, I spend 15 minutes meditating. A great book on this subject is Russell Simmons's SUCCESS THROUGH STILLNESS. You can listen to the audio book on your walk.

I've tried countless morning rituals. I've tried exercising, I've tried affirmations, I've tried just jumping right in and getting busy, then taking a nap later. That worked okay but it didn't help my jeans fit any better. So far, walk and a book, meditation, and lemon water at work (I'm still drinking coffee in the morning while I write and you can't stop me!) has shown me more serious benefits than anything else I've ever tried to start my day on the right foot. And if nothing else, it's gonna be cold sooner or later, so I might as well enjoy some sunshine while I can; God knows winter is coming.

If you're a writer, trust me, you NEED to get off your ass and move your body. And for the lives we lead, an aerobic workout is best. You don't need abs of steel, you need a body and mind that's in it for the long haul.

20. 6 TIPS FOR WRITERS IN RELATIONSHIPS.

• • • •

HOW IS YOUR RELATIONSHIP with your significant other? With your kids? With your friends? As writers, we spend so much time in our heads, our relationships with the people who matter most to us often begin to suffer. I can't tell you how many times I've heard, "What's wrong with you?" only to reply, "Nothing," and mean it. Because there wasn't anything wrong. I was just in my head, working through whatever I was writing at the time, trying on an ending or searching for the right title.

It's unfortunate for the people we care about, but we can't help it. We live in a make-believe world most of the time, but it's a world WE'RE responsible for and what kind of god would we be if we stopped paying attention to the small details? And then someone at work pipes up and says, "What are you in such a bad mood for?"

"Um ... I'm not?"

"Well, you look like you are."

"Nope. Perfectly fine." I was just trying to decide if the main character should die in the end or defeat the monster. Do you think this title gives too much away, or is it mysterious and exotic?

And I'm by NO means a relationship expert. Good Christ, just the thought of it. It's downright laughable. I've gone months without talking to friends before, even my closest friends, but when I do talk to them again, it's like no time has passed at all. And, sure, the phone works both ways, but also the phone works BOTH WAYS. And one of those ways was mine and I neglected it because I was so busy writing one short story after another, or I got so deep into a novel I forgot a birthday. It's unfortunate, but it happens.

Luckily there are steps we can take to help strengthen those bonds and at least look like we're trying. Again, I'm no expert. But I do know how to read and find out the things I know nothing about. So here goes:

1) I've mentioned before knowing a person's rules and communicating yours to them and how important this is. I can't stress it enough. I have a friend who, a long time ago, I got home from work one day and he had opened my mail while waiting for me because we had plans that night. I guess in most cases I would have shrugged it off, but this time it was a rejection letter. I've gotten tons of them since then, but this was my very first rejection letter from my very first submission. Man, that's a feeling you face alone the first time. Eventually you get over it and it's nothing anymore, but I was 19, had been writing about a year and a half at the time, and was not ready to share that kind of stuff just yet. His only comment was, "I didn't know you were submitting work." Maybe there's a reason for that. But, you know what? I couldn't really get mad at him. Because his rules for things weren't the same as mine. He didn't and never has valued his privacy the way I do mine, so he didn't know. It really did something to our friendship, but it probably hurt it even worse that I kept quiet about it and just went on with my day, a little damaged and untrusting and possibly even more protective of my privacy after that. Of course, at the time I had no idea how to communicate and didn't even have the words for what I was feeling. If I HAD, and if I'd told him about it, things could have gone different. We're still friends, we always will be, but there's a little part of me that will never forget that. And that's on me.

2) I think the reason my friends and I get along so well, the reason we can go so long apart and then talk again like we just talked yesterday, is because we expect nothing from each other. I'm not friends with any of these people because I'm trying to get something from them. If anything, I want to do whatever I can FOR them. If you build your

relationships on what you can get rather than what you can give, you're headed in the wrong direction for sure.

3) When you meet resistance in a relationship, confront it then. Don't wait. Resistance leads to Resentment leads to Rejection leads to Repression (see #1 above). We're not always going to agree but keeping your mouth shut and eating it ... well, it's going to start eating YOU from the inside. Our relationships work best when WE'RE at our best.

4) This is the one we writers have the most trouble with. You have to make your relationships a priority. You remember that part in FIGHT CLUB where the narrator is talking about "the couch problem"? You get the new couch and you say to yourself, Okay, I've got that couch problem solved, and you move on and never again have to worry about the couch. Christ, this is my entire life. I make a friend. Okay, I got that friend problem solved, now I can get back to what I was doing before. We keep people at a distance because we've got this novel we're working on and we really want to finish it, so we'll do something in a couple weeks, cool? That's not how you build a relationship, that's how you build an acquaintanceship!

5) Do the work. With friends, try to do one thing every week to make the friendship better. Go get coffee or see a movie. Have a conversation, even if it's only over text because you're several states away and you both have busy lives. I have a book called THE BOOK OF USELESS INFORMATION. Every morning I text a handful of my closest friends one bit of useless trivia from that book. Today it was: "Lachanophobia is the fear of vegetables." A couple of friends I share music with every morning. Another friend and I swap music every Thursday. It's a weekly ritual. When we both remember. But even when we forget, we get it the next week without missing a beat. That's friendship. With a relationship, a spouse or your kids, you don't TRY to do something, you DO something. With my kids, we share comics. I still buy my younger son and daughter comics every month when I buy my own haul. And sometimes I read theirs before handing them

over. My daughter and I (she's the only one still living at home, so it's just easier with her) have spaghetti and/or pizza once a week and do the grocery shopping together every other weekend. In fact, she goes with me pretty much every time I leave the house. Sometimes we just go to the guitar store to see what's new and ogle the beautiful guitars. Sometimes this means I cut my writing short for the day, but she's 18 and won't be around forever, so I'm trying to make sure those bonds are unbreakable. I didn't do this with the boys when I should have, because I was too wrapped up in my own head. I'm trying to make the efforts NOW, of course, but I regret not doing it sooner.

6) Remind yourself why this person and this relationship matters to you. I bought a little 2X3 notebook for, like, $1, and every morning I write something in it that I'm grateful for. This would be a good place to remind myself why my family and friends are important to me. Keeping these things in mind helps us to make them a priority. It is SO easy for writers to put their relationships on the back burner and not give it a second thought and that's an excellent way to lose a friend or, worse, a spouse. Yes, the work is important and we want to get it done, but even the most hardened antisocial misfit in the world needs someone to talk to now and then.

Don't let the writing make you lose sight of all the other things you have in your life, all the people whose lives your presence—or your ABSENCE—affects.

21. THE WORLD OWES ME A LIVING AND I INTEND TO COLLECT

• • • •

THE BIBLE SAYS "LOVE of money is the root of all evil." But I like Prince's thoughts on the matter better. He said, "They say money don't happiness, but it'll pay for the search."

Damn right.

Money is the bane of the writer's—hell, all creators'—existence. We NEED it to survive, but we'd do this thing even if we knew going in we were never going to make a dime at it. We don't do it for the money, we do it because we love it that much. But think how much more time we'd have to do it if we didn't have those damn day jobs. So, to cast off the day job, we have to make money with our art. Which can be a hard issue to press when, really, we just want to be seen and heard whether we're getting paid or not. I can't tell you the number of free books I've given out because I'm just so pleased with the books and want other people to read them. And yet I hate my day job and wish to God I made enough money from writing to not have to work one anymore.

All hope is not lost, though. There are several tips for making money that can be adapted to writers. At least, I hope they can. Let's see what we've got.

1) Create Wealth. What this means is, whatever you do, fiction, painting, music, films, find a way to do it that adds value to the lives of your audience. For myself, I try like hell to write stories that reward readers who go in for a second round. I want my fiction to read even better the second time through. I want readers to pick up new details, new words or turns of phrase they didn't catch the first time that can, in retrospect, make the experience even more enjoyable the second time.

My short story "The Timesmiths", I think, works like this, if a reader is paying attention. I think my short story, "Monday", does it too, even better. And I hope an upcoming short, "Problems and Bigger Ones" does the same, too. I try to slip in phrases or actions that work well for the narrative the first time, but if they read it again, they might say OH, I see what he was doing, yeah yeah, that makes it even better.

Does this add value? I don't know about that, but I like to think paying for a story once and getting more and more enjoyment out of it the MORE times your read it adds value.

Also: maximize your work's potential. Writers of fiction, we can do audio books and add value that way. Musicians can license their music—some local business might want to use one of your songs in a commercial. Filmmakers can gather together with other local filmmakers and hold their own film festival.

2) Maintain Your Wealth. You've probably heard it said many times before, "spend less than you earn and invest the difference." What I like to do—and this may or may not work for you; I don't know your situation—is ... I have a day job (night job), so I get a regular paycheck from that, and that's enough to cover my bills and allow me to buy comics and go out to eat and see movies now and then. I don't rely on money from writing. And thank God for that, because I'd be dead in a ditch somewhere if I did. So what I do is, my regular paycheck goes into my checking account. But anything I make from writing goes into my SAVINGS account. My Visa is not tied to my savings account. Sure, I can transfer money from one to the other with a phone call, but that's a hassle usually, so the savings account money just sits there and collects. And as for reinvesting, when you have enough built up, use that money and invest it in your writing. Buy a professional cover, hire an editor, pay for some ads. When you're still at that stage where you're trying to make it in the business, it's a good idea to use at least part of what you make from your art and put it back into the business in some way that expands your reach and gets your stuff out there to more people, or

helps you to improve the quality of upcoming works. Investing in your career is VITAL because, at this stage, you can't rely on others to do it for you.

3) Increase Your Wealth: Reinvest. When your initial investment pays off, the book you bought the fancy cover for starts selling, or you bought some new software that improves the quality of your films or music, reinvest that money back into your business again. Hell, I shouldn't even have to tell you this, because you're already investing in yourself, so naturally why would you NOT reinvest when you start making real money? Well, because people sometimes lose sight of their goals. Especially when you've spent most of your adult life living paycheck to paycheck. Seeing that new balance in your savings account can get the wheels turning. Trust me, you WILL start seeing things you like in a new light. You WILL start thinking "You know, if I wanted to, right now, I could buy that. I have the money." But let's be real, you don't need it. It's gonna satisfy a very brief itch and tomorrow that money will still be gone.

4) Enjoy Your Wealth: Look, I'm not saying NEVER spend any of the money you've made, but follow the first few steps FIRST, and then enjoy the spoils. As long as you remember the most important rule of spending LESS than you earn. You deserve a present now and then. Or someone you love deserves a present. The psychological effects of treating yourself to something you've had your eye on can do wonders for your state of mind and self esteem sometimes—especially knowing you were able to do this, whatever the gift is, from your own hard work and talent. Myself, I'm a comic book junkie. If I've had a lean month or something else has come up, something with the kids or whatever, I won't buy more than my regular monthly haul. But if I've got a little extra in the bank and I've taken care of what needs taken care of first, I'll buy a couple of back issues I've been looking for. But NEVER if I can't afford it. But you have to learn how to flip that switch between something you NEED to survive and something you

just WANT because you think it'll enhance your life. Know what will REALLY enhance your life? Having the money later in life to take care of yourself. I work with a guy who turned 71 this year!!! I don't want to be that guy. So I can't spend more than I earn, and I need to make sure I've got some put away.

This topic might not be for everybody, but I do believe MOST of the creators I know, that's what they want to do with their life full time. I'm not guaranteeing that if you follow these steps, you'll wake up tomorrow to a full bank account, but what I can promise is that following these steps, living by these steps, will go a hell of a lot further toward financial independence than blowing all your money on payday and then trying to do those financial gymnastic we've all done, trying to figure out how many more weeks you can put off THIS bill, what number do you call to make an arrangement for THAT bill.

I'm with Prince on this one, I know money won't make me happy, but it'll sure as hell help me figure out what will.

22. HAVE YOU RAISED YOUR STANDARDS TODAY?

. . . .

I ALWAYS LIKE IT WHEN Gordon Ramsey gets pissed at some young chef for not raising their standards and letting less than perfect food onto the plate. Every time it happens on HELL'S KITCHEN or KITCHEN NIGHTMARES or MASTER CHEF, I think about writing and how often I've let a story go out with a less than perfect ending or a sub-par edit. And then I think about how I feel knowing that work is out there.

We're definitely a "good enough" society these days. So many new authors out there who weren't around in the days of submissions and rejections and Writer's Markets and response times and guidelines and SASE (I'm not even going to explain what that means because as a writer YOU SHOULD ALREADY KNOW!) think it's nothing at all, this writing thing. Hammer out a 40,000 word "novel" in a few days, give it a quick read-through, slap a cover on it, and quit your day job.

See, they don't have standards, because they never learned to develop them.

But like Sean Nelson said, "Only cream and bastards rise," so my job now is to be that cream that rises to the top. While all the Seanny-Come-Latelies (Bain knows what I'm talking about!) are pumping out a new "unit" every two weeks, I'm going to craft my stories with care. Which I've always tried to do anyway, but I do admit now and then to tacking on an ending just for the sake of an ending. But what's the rush?

We're not under deadlines anymore, unless you're foolish enough to submit your upcoming book for pre-sale. But miss that deadline and no more pre-sales for you. So why are we trying to hurry and get more and more work out there? I'll tell you why. Greed. The same reason my bosses at my day job can't be satisfied with meeting the schedule and feel the need to add to it every time we might finish a little early. It's not needed, but think of the money! And then we end up spending a week off work without pay because SOMEONE over-produced. But I digress.

Why this constant rush to get out a new book every week or every two weeks when all we're doing is sacrificing quality for quantity. Two years ago I pushed to put out a new title every month for a year. And I did it. But I'm the first to admit not every one of those titles was great. Some came to be because I needed an idea I could finish within that month. That's not to say I think any of them are terrible, but I had one or two that weren't my best work, and could have been made a lot better with a little more time and care given to them.

But I sacrificed standards in favor of just getting it out there.

No more.

From now on I'll live and write by a code.

1) There's no rush. As in the old days, a story is done when it's done NOT when I decide it's been too long since I've published anything new and I need to get something out there to keep my name in readers' minds.

2) I'm not going to concern myself with what other writers are doing, whether they're more successful for not. I'm not them, I can't write their work, but also they can't write mine. So I need only be true to myself and the work that I do.

3) Do my best, each and every day. When I sit down to the keyboard, I'm not putting down words for the sake of putting down words, but also neither am I dilly-dallying around because I "don't feel like it." I've put in enough hours behind the desk to know that, if I really WANT to, I can write new words EVERY DAY. THAT is me at my best.

4) Every day I will appreciate the gifts I've been given. My life, my family, my writing, my friends. As much as I complain, I really do have a good life. I should spend a little more time appreciating it.

This is just a start. I can add to this list as they come to me, the important thing is to be able to look at myself every day and know I lived up the standards I set for myself and my work. What standards have you set for yourself and how strict are you in keeping—or better yet, RAISING—them?

23. TIME...HE'S WAITING IN THE WINGS, HE SPEAKS OF SENSELESS THINGS

· · · ·

I FEEL LIKE I'VE TALKED about this before, but for writers with a day job, time management cannot be stressed enough.

I'm currently fortunate in that I have from roughly 8 AM to 2 PM every day to write, if I want to. I don't actually spend this much time writing, but I have in the past and I loved every second of it. But now my daughter is graduated and home most of the day and I like to spend time with her. I've got my walks to take, and when the grandkids are here, I want to spend time with them, too. Also, when you have another job you have to go to, spending all day at the keyboard and getting NOTHING else done is not only mentally exhausting, but sooner or later you'll look around and realize I REALLY need to dust and vacuum.

So I allot a solid TWO HOUR block for writing new words. This is the time I used to spend writing when I worked a day job and got up at 4:00 every morning to write before work. Two hours is a good deal of time to make some solid progress on the current project, and at the end of it I'm still riding that writing high and wishing I could stay and do it all night. That's a good feeling to carry around because it makes rousing myself and getting back to the computer the next day just a little easier.

I also give myself 30-45 minutes to do a blog entry, but that's current and I don't honestly know how long I'll keep that up. I'd like to say indefinitely, but, well... We'll see. For now, though, I write for two hours, then do a blog post, then get away from my desk and spend time with my daughter. That's a 6 hour block of time I COULD be writing and I never feel like it's enough time, even if I'd written THE END on something that day and have no desire nor plans to start anything else just yet. I have a feeling it's like that for most writers. We just want to write, no matter what else is going on around us. The call of the keys...

And I understand that not every writer out there has that kind of time. Hell, I want nothing more than to get on day shift at my current job, knowing full well that eliminates my day long writing schedule. And I'm fine with that. Because I'll just go back to 2 hours a day and I'll do what I did for the 13 years before that: make it work.

Because I know how to manage my time. Wanna know a secret? I'm a Time Lord. I can take time and bend it, stretch it, wrap it around, and generally distort it however I like. I'm not alone, though. I bet you could do it, too. Ever been so engrossed in something you enjoy that you happen to glance at the clock a few minutes later and find it's really five HOURS later? Yeah, you have!

We use this distortion technique every day in one way or another. You ever go somewhere for the first time and it seems to take forever, but the more times you go there, it seems the shorter the trip is? Or how about when you're driving outside of town and, again, it takes FOR! EVER! But the return trip HOME always seems to go by much quicker, even though you're driving the exact same distance.

Time distortion, y'all. And we can apply this to our writing schedule and make that thirty minutes you have free feel like two hours or more.

First, you have to alter your beliefs about time. How long is a minute? How long is an hour? How long is a day? A week? A month? You get the idea. Remember in school when we had to do that fluoride rinse once a week? Only took 60 seconds but the stuff was so foul it was the longest minute of the day. But recess, which was, what 30 minutes? SNAP, over like that.

Because we hated the fluoride rinse and were focusing only on THAT and getting it out of our mouths, time dragged on and on and on and on and on. But at recess, you were having a blast and not even considering what time it was.

See, a minute isn't really any time at all. And thirty minutes, you can get a LOT of stuff done in that time. Because you've gained a lifetime's worth of experience with minutes and half hours, we have certain beliefs about how long each of those is. Same with an hour, a day, etc.

Do me a favor. Open a book, any book, and set it next to you on your desk. Now spend the next FIVE MINUTES copying the text of that book into a blank page on your computer. Don't worry about accuracy, just copy what you see as best you can. Now at the end of that five minutes, do a word count to see just how many words you typed in only five minutes.

I guarantee it was a few hundred, if not more. Look at how many words you can write in FIVE MINUTES. Didn't think that was possible did you? Because you see five minutes as a blink, as nothing compared to all the other measurements of time you use throughout the day.

Imagine how many words you could type in thirty minutes. Or TWO HOURS. Confession, the most I've written in one two-hour session was over 4000 words. It was a long time ago, it only happened once at the end of a project, and I've never been able to duplicate it, although I've come close several times.

Okay, now that we've altered your beliefs about time, we have to distort your *perception* of time.

You've got an hour to write before you HAVE to get the kids up for school, get them FROM school, or start dinner. Whatever the upcoming task that's keeping you from just writing long into the night, how do you make it feel like twice as much time, or four times as much time, without actually taking that much time?

Sometimes I write with the pomodoro method. That's a focused 25 minutes of writing, then a 5 minute break, then another 25 minutes of writing followed by another 5 minute break, alternating until I make it stop. The problem with this method—and I use it a lot, but then I have 6 hours a day I can do this if I want to—is that it forces you to focus too much on how much time has passed vs. how much time is left. You need to be able to concentrate on your writing WITHOUT the constant countdown. On my phone, I have several alarms set. One for 8:30. One for 10:00. One for 11:00. And one at 2:15. This is my drop everything and get ready for work alarm. The 8:30 alarm is the "it's about time to start heading back home from the walk because it's going to be time to write soon" alarm. 10:00 is the "you need to start writing" alarm. 11:00 is the "you've been writing for an hour, how much have you got done?" alarm. I know these alarms are there, but there's no countdown, no worry of a random alarm signaling time to take a break when I'm just getting into the heart of a scene. I can take my time, I can stretch my literary wings, so to speak, and just let it flow. The alarm will sound when it's time to, but when it does it's only the "just checking in to see how you're doing" alarm, no big deal.

And you know what happens? Amazing things. Since the countdown is the last thing I'm worried about, it's the last thing I worry about, and that hour until the next alarm can feel like several hours. This morning I wrote the day's 1034 words in 28 minutes!!!

God, can you imagine if I'd been doing the pomodoro and 25 minutes in, the timer beeps and I lose the flow right there at the end. Don't get me wrong, like I said, I love the pomodoro method. But it's not for every writing situation or writing session. Sometimes just knowing that countdown is happening right next to you can be enough to keep you from putting down ANY words that day.

So I forego that and just write, knowing my hour alarms will keep me posted on the time. That's another thing, do NOT look to see what time it is once you've started. I know normally a watched clock never moves, but when you're writing and watching the clock at the same time, the blank page never fills.

Okay, we've changed your beliefs about time, and we've seen how you can distort the advance of time. Last step: Prioritize your tasks!

I have several things I want to get done every day. Things IN ADDITION to that day's words and that day's blog post. But those are the two most important, and that day's words are THE most important. So I do that first. Every day. There are days I don't even answer emails until after the day's words are done. You can do a dozen smaller tasks during the same amount of time you would have spent writing, but when that time is over, did you really do anything IMPORTANT?

Do the important things first, so that at the end of that time, or at the end of the day, you can look back and know you didn't waste whatever time you had. Once the day's words and the day's blog post are done, it's time to start digging into those other, smaller, tasks. THIS is when you play with new cover designs or re-work your calls to action or send out a welcome email to your new newsletter subscribers. All worthwhile tasks for the self-publishing author, but without getting those new words done, there's not going to be anything new to self publish.

All daily schedules are not built the same. I don't know your situation or how much time you have every day to get some writing done, but I DO know that, using these few techniques, you CAN get some writing done, and chances are you'll get more done than you first thought you could. Once you start to understand just how much is possible to do in a short amount of time and once you stop focusing on how much time is passing vs. how much time is left, you can prioritize that time to get maximum results and help your career advance one writing session at a time.

24. "WHY SO SERIOUS?"—THE JOKER

. . . .

WHO SAID WRITING HAS to be nothing but words words words every day? Sure, we have no problem with that. But every so often, it's good to take a day off and purposely NOT write anything. Just don't make a habit of it.

It is very possible to get burned out, so it's important that you take a step back BEFORE that happens, otherwise that one day off can turn into two days and soon a week, then a month and before you know it you haven't written anything in 6 months and now you feel like it's been so long, you're not sure you even know how to do it still.

So it's not a terrible idea to take a day off now and then. But this is important: do NOT take that day off between projects. That's when it's easiest to let the days off multiply. Take a day off when you're right in the middle of something and you're having a blast working on it. That way you'll want to come back to it the day after.

Writing is a solitary pursuit. I don't care how many writer friends you have, how many writers' groups you belong to, or how many subscribers to your newsletter. When you sit down and face that page, you're all by yourself. So every now and then you need to push away from the desk, stand up, go talk to other people, step outside and get some sunshine on your face.

Or sometimes maybe you just need a day off from the current work. This can be fun and constructive, too. Usually in the middle of a novel, I find I can keep my focus by stepping away for a couple of days and writing a short story instead. This way I'm still writing, but I'm not wearing out the welcome on the novel, and those few days away usually makes me eager to get back to work on it.

Or just try some random writing. A good writing prompt book works well for this. 642 Things to Write About is an excellent start. This is the prompt book I have and I'm enjoying it a lot.

Have fun with the projects you choose. I'm currently several titles in on a series of short stories based on making every calendar holiday into a horror story, inspired by the great slasher movies I grew up with, like April Fool's Day and Mother's Day. It's fun and inspiring to try to turn every new holiday into a workable horror story, but I think so far I'm managing pretty well. Or find inspiration in other places. I've also got a few titles in on a series of Angel Hill shorts, each one based on the title of a Harvey Danger song because I think they have excellent titles and they make me think.

Have fun with your characters. I once named a couple of characters Seamoon and Toomey because, when I was writing the story ("Coming Down the Mountain"), I was listening to Paul McCartney's song "C-Moon", which has the line "C-Moon, to me." It was a silly way to name my characters, but it worked and it's almost 20 years later and I still remember it.

Writing is an art and you should definitely give it the respect it deserves, especially in the new landscape of the self-published author. But, Christ, you still need to enjoy your life, right? Take it seriously, but not so seriously you drain all the enjoyment out of it and start seeing it as a chore. Writing was never meant to be a chore. Those of us who do it, who did it in the days before you could just throw something up online and call yourself a published author, we did it because we love it. That's the attitude you have to have. Do it because you love it. And if there comes a day when you don't love it anymore, take a step back, take a day off and go to the park or go for a long drive with some great music blasting. Go watch a movie with your family. Grill something and eat outside (I just had lunch on the porch swing with my daughter, a frozen pizza, and it was wonderful). And when the work starts to bog you down, turn the tables. Grab a random line of dialogue from television or a book and write a funny 1000 word story based just on that one line.

No matter how seriously you take this, never forget to live your life and to have fun in everything you do. Anything less is no way to live.

25. HOW TO BE THE HERO OF YOUR OWN STORY.

• • • •

I'VE GOT THIS FRIEND who works with troubled kids. That's her job. But in her community there are other troubled kids whose problems don't fall within the parameters of her job. These kids don't NEED help, but help would be appreciated. But how to do what needs to be done within a system that says these kids don't need that kind of help? Well, do it anyway. After all, you do a thing enough times and, even if it's not the way things were always done, eventually it becomes the way things are done. And no one even saw it coming.

But it's a risk, isn't it? To go against the norm and charge ahead anyway? I read something today that I felt summed it up pretty nicely. "If you want to play the game and WIN, you've got to be play 'full out.' You've got to be willing to feel stupid, and you've got to be willing to try things that might not work—and if they don't work, be willing to change your approach. Otherwise, how could you innovate, how could you grow, how could you discover who you really are?"

For more years than I've been alive, it was the common belief among the writing community that self publishing was the sign of either an amateur or a really terrible writer. And now it's just the way it is. People are turning to self publishing every day, and some people are making an incredible living at it. But ten years ago if you'd floated that idea, you'd have been laughed out of the message board. TRADITIONAL was the only way to publish. The only ACCEPTED way to publish.

But I knew in 2001 or 2002 that self publishing FELT like a viable option. After all, if all you're looking to do is get your work to readers who want to read it, why can't you just sell it directly to them? It's stupid to think that's impossible, but that's how people felt back then.

I just can't see doing everything the way "everyone" says it "should" be done. WHY should it be done that way? WHO says? Life is short and if you're not charging ahead and forging your own path to achieve the things you want to achieve before the icy fingers of death take you in their cold embrace, what the hell are you living for?

What kind of person just does everything he's told the way he's told to do it?

If you want to be a writer but have always lacked the confidence or the know-how, speak now or FOREVER hold your peace. Because there's no time to waste. And writing ... no one is great at it right out of the gate, talent takes time to develop, so get started NOW. Your first works are going to be bad, but if you're "in it to win it" and you commit to the process and the craft, you will get better.

I know a LOT of writers and I'd say less than half of them have any sort of formal education in creative writing. God knows I don't. I learned as I went (and I'm still learning). The ones who don't, they had an idea and they wrote it. Simple as that. It could have been terrible. It probably was. But they did it again with another one after that, and another one after that, and pretty soon they wrote something and gave it to someone to read and that person said "Whoa, this is really good!"

So don't come to me and say I want to write, but I don't know how. NONE of us know how at first. All we knew was there was this idea and it wanted to come out. We're all stumbling along in the dark at first. Hell, that's kind of what makes it so much fun. And you get to experience that exciting fear every time, because the thrill of creation never goes away as long as you stay in love with writing. Or whatever form of expression your creative desires take.

Honestly, I don't know what you're waiting for. You want to do it, you know you want to do it, so stop being a wimp and just write something. Anything. I can only hold your hand so long, but the real work is all yours to do.

Get the words down and come back later for the education. Write your first few stories, get comfortable with the process, and once you are, then come back and read things like THE ELEMENTS OF STYLE and ZEN IN THE ART OF WRITING. Read King's ON WRITING. Read King. Read everyone. Read. And write. Write every day. Write with all your heart. Write as if your life depends on it. Write like there's no tomorrow. Write like it's the only thing in your life that matters because, trust me, there will be days when it is.

Don't write for me, don't write for an audience, not at first. Just write for you. Prince once said if he can please himself musically, he knows he can please others, and that's how I look at my writing. If I'm happy with it, that happiness with shine through and it will connect with others as well.

And when you get started, don't settle for telling the same old stories in the same old way. Create new stories, and new ways to tell them. Don't think that's possible? Read HOUSE OF LEAVES by Mark Danielewski and then tell me there are no new ways to tell a story.

You're not writing to fit in or to be in the middle of the pack. I know I'm not. I'm writing to be the best. And I hope you are too. There's plenty of room for everyone at the top and a little friendly competition never hurt anyone. Well, that Jan and Dean guy, but, you know...

My point is, once you get started, don't look to others to tell you how things should be done. YOU decide how things should be done. It's YOUR path. You forge it however you want.

Now stop reading motivational books all day and GO WRITE.

Thank you for reading this book. I hope you will consider leaving an honest review.

• • • •

IF YOU WOULD LIKE TO keep up to date on my writing and where it can be found, why not join my FREE weekly newsletter HERE[1].

---

1. https://cdennismoore.us3.list-manage.com/

subscribe?u=98166cbe6a6ccf1d7a39e772e&id=ac9e73819c

Don't miss out!

Visit the website below and you can sign up to receive emails whenever C. Dennis Moore publishes a new book. There's no charge and no obligation.

https://books2read.com/r/B-A-EPXB-UFGR

BOOKS 2 READ

Connecting independent readers to independent writers.

Did you love *Doing it Write*? Then you should read *Shut Up and Write*[2] by C. Dennis Moore!

[3]

Do you have a novel in you that won't come out? Do you dream of writing but can't find the motivation or inspiration? Are you intimidated by all the successful authors out there to the point you want to give up and think "Why me?"**Why NOT you?**That's the question SHUT UP AND WRITE asks and answers.This book is designed to help the struggling writer, no matter how far along in their journey, find their passion and confidence to sit down and put words on a page on a consistent basis.Through examples and experience spanning three decades, author C. Dennis Moore leads the reader through a series of trials and tribulations, from how to overcome the fear of failure to having the faith to take those first steps on your literary

---

2. https://books2read.com/u/b6Lr2y

3. https://books2read.com/u/b6Lr2y

journey.Other topics include efficiency, productivity, morning rituals, finding your audience of one, and honoring your influences. SHUT UP AND WRITE is for all writers, all styles, and all genres.**If you dream of seeing your name on the cover of a book but have been letting fear or doubt get in your way, SHUT UP AND WRITE was made for you.**

About the Author

C. Dennis Moore is the author of the Angel Hill novels, the Monsters of Green Lake series, as well as the Holiday Horrors. He lives in St. Joseph, MO with his wife, Kara. They have seven children and three grandchildren.